MICKEY

The story of a boy growing up on Vancouver Island

Mike Gogo

Canadian Cataloguing in Publication Data
Gogo, Mike, 1945-, author
Mickey : the story of a boy growing up on Vancouver Island / Mike Gogo.

ISBN 978-0-9920661-0-9 (pbk.)

1. Gogo, Mike, 1945- --Childhood and youth. 2. Vancouver Island
(B.C.)--Biography. I. Title.

FC3844.3.G64A3 2013   971.1'204092
C2013-905320-4

Typing and Typeset: Karen Gogo, Sue Palmer

and Wanda Corkill

Assistance in layout: Rose Roy

Photo Retouching: Lenore Hayes

Photographs courtesy of: Gogo Family Archives

Publication Assistance (and cartooning): Paul Roland Gogo

...also available FRANK NEY *A Canadian Legend*

ISBN 0-9699468-0-5 (Gogo@Trooper.com)

For any correspondence or for copies of this book:

mikegogo@shaw.ca

Mike Gogo

2625 South Forks Rd .

Nanaimo, British Columbia

Canada

V9X-1H3

FIRST EDITION

This book is a 100% Canadian Product.

NO public funds (Grants) were used in the making of this book

*"Everybody wants to go to heaven
but nobody wants to die."*

Joe Louis

CONTENTS

2	MY GRANDFATHER'S HANDS
4	DRAIN THE BOAT
8	GOING TO SCHOOL WITH MY SISTER MARJORIE
8	IRENE
9	BOOTLEGGING AT SCHOOL AND LEGION DANCES
11	GOOD OLD MILLY
12	WELFARE IN UNIFORM
14	GOOD OLD ERIC
16	SWEET MARIE
21	MY UNCLE GEORGE GIVING ME 50 CENTS
22	MY BROTHER EDDY BEATING UP TWO BOYS
23	SISTER SUPERIOR AND THE PHONE CALL TO MY HOME
24	KISSING BETTY THROUGH THE FLY SCREEN
25	LITTLE ANTHONY AND THE FLOOR WAX
25	PUKING IN CHURCH
26	BIG EDDY GALANT
26	THE JOYS OF FARTING ON YOUR BROTHER
27	MY SAFE AND STRUCTURED CHILDHOOD
28	TOMBOLA TICKETS
29	BEAUTIFUL ROMANO BORTOLOTTO
30	FATHER HANLY AND THE CROSS
31	CHRIS THE BULLY
31	HUMMINGBIRDS
32	WHATEVER HAPPENED TO LENNIE DAGALIEZ?
32	STEALING BANANAS FROM THE DUTCHMAN
33	THE MUSIC TEACHER AND THE THIEVING ALTER BOY
34	COULD BUY IT AT THE CONVENT FOR 5 CENTS
36	THE TINY NUN SAYING "YOU'RE THE BAD ONE"
36	STEALING IS OUR ALLOWANCE
37	NOBODY HAS 8 KIDS!
40	PRETTY LITTLE SHIRLEY
40	SISTER SUPERIOR
41	HOW TO CREATE A BOMB "THE BASANELLOS"
42	MR. CARL ANDERSON
43	LOUIS TOGNELLO
44	KILLING THE GOAT
44	HOW TO MAKE IT PAY CUTTING HAY
45	TARZAN
46	THE BROPHY'S
48	LOOSING MY VIRGINITY
49	THE GOOD LAWYER
50	STEALING COINS FROM THE JAM CAN

51	THE BIG CHANGE
55	BARE BALLS IN THE RIVER
57	DEANNA MCINTYRE
59	MY AUNTIE BERTHA
60	THE POLICE CORPORAL AND THE MISSING CATS
61	THE LACROSSE PLAYING PEACH STEALERS
62	FENCE PICKETS AND BLACK BAKED POTATOES
62	TOMMY AND LENNY
63	MR DUNCAN'S OUTHOUSE
63	DON'T SHOOT THE PHEASANT
64	DON'T PISS THE BED
64	FISHING AND BEE STINGS
65	HALF CRUCIFIED IN THE HAY BARN
66	I LOVE CHRISTMAS
66	EARL THE GYPSY
67	SHOOTING THE OWL
68	MEXICAN CREDIT CARD
69	STEALING BLACKBERRIES AT MR.MIROSLAVES
70	RAFTING ON THE CREEK
70	CAROL'S UNDERPANTS ON THE CLOTHESLINE
71	MY SISTER LAURA AND THE GIBSON GIRLS
72	THE BEST FRIEND EVER "MAD DOG"
75	MY FIRST DEER
76	GRANDPA'S CABIN
78	BETTER GET YOUR EYES CHECKED POPCORN
79	BYE BYE "IKE" THE BULLDOG
80	THE GOLD PANNER
80	MEL SAVES MY ASS
81	A BOY WHO LOVED FISHING
82	HOW I GOT TO TOWN
83	OUTRUNNING THE COPS
83	SONNY
84	PISSING IN THE VAPOUR PAN
85	PATIENT CATHY AND LUCIEN THE ASSHOLE
86	DAVY AND MONZI
86	WHERE IS JOE CATULOW
88	LIFE ON THE FARM
89	I CANT MAKE SOUP OUT OF TRACKS
90	THEFT AT THE #14 HOUSE
92	POP HAWKINS
96	NOT SAFE SEX
96	5 CENTS A GAME
97	THE CHOCOLATE MILK MAN
98	DRUGS
99	THE HORNEY GIRL AND MY BELT
101	DAD KICKS MY PUNK ASS
102	"DODIE" AS CLOSE TO A SAINT AS I HAVE EVER KNOWN

Dedicated to:

I wrote this book so that my descendants could read what my life was like when I was a boy. The book is dedicated to my brother Ed who helped me out so many times when I started contract logging. Love ya Tatey. To my brother Ken who taught me how to operate equipment. To my sister Marjorie who taught me how to bully and manipulate people, that sure came in handy. To my brother Ron who set the bar in honesty and compassion way too high for me to ever live up to. To my sister Marilyn who once told me "life is what you make it" I have never forgotten that advice. To my brother, Ed for always being there for me. To my sister Laura for her humor and silliness; always a good laugh with her. To my brother Dan for putting up with my tenacity and madness when we were kids. I wish we could all sit around the Christmas tree once more at our Fifth Street home.

*Mickey and Danny in the backyard
– note the barbed wire*

MY GRANDFATHER'S HANDS

Think hard now. What is the first thing that you remember growing up? Think hard. For me it was looking up at my grandfather's hands when I was 3 years old. Sadly that is the year he died, so I didn't remember his face just the hands beside a cane on a wicker rocking chair. Although I will admire him until hell will not have it, I only truly appreciated him one winter's day, a year ago, when the power went off and I was sitting in a cold living room realizing that I had no heat, water or light. I thought of how my grandfather lived 10 miles from a town and all the lonely nights he spent on the farm. He worked every day of his life. Bullshit, you say, but he was not the only one, as most pioneer farmers on Vancouver Island worked in a coal mine or on a logging or sawmilling site. They would put in their long, hard and dangerous work day, then come home to unharness their horse and milk cows, feed chickens and slop the pigs and then make their own supper and something for their next day's lunch, sick or not. He married a woman whose husband had been assassinated because he was a union leader. They only lived together for about five years when she left her son and husband high and dry to go to the World's fair and never came back for 40 years. My father told me the hardest thing that he ever had to do was tell his mother to hit the road as, by the time she came back, his father was 87 and lived with him, so he was not about to subject his father to her presence. How sad is that? Hard times tough people. I can understand her not wanting to endure the hardships of pioneer life but to leave her 4 sons from a previous man and her 5 year old with my grandfather and walk out was not cool. But in fairness, I do not, nor will not, ever know her side of the story. My father and my grandfather both died when they were 88, neither one from any disease but only old age. You gotta love those genetics.

Dan Gogo and Mike (Mickey) Gogo

DRAIN
THE BOAT

When my older brother Dan and I were 6 and 7 years old we used to sit in a beautiful canoe that was owned by my older brother Ron. One day in warm weather he half filled the boat with water to keep the wood swelled up and tight. Of course we had no clue as to why the boat had water in it, so we tried to flip it over to drain it so we could sit in it once again. The boat was too heavy for us to flip, and thinking the boat should not have water in it, we got a pickaxe out of the basement and put a dozen holes in it to drain it. Well my brother Ron came home from work and of course went postal on us. He told our father and all the old man could do was laugh and say "isn't that just like a kid" and as usual we were not punished.

Ron pushed logs around all day in a lake with a pike pole and he had abs beyond belief. He let Dan and I punch him in the gut until we tired out. This went on until he got married and moved out of the house.

He was a sweetheart and an unbelievably generous man. I once saw him meet a man on the street that he knew from years gone by. He asked the man how he was doing and the man told Ron that he had lost his job and was cutting and selling firewood to get by. Ron told him to bring him 3 cords, even though his backyard was full. I talked to a man at Ron's funeral and asked him how he knew Ron, he told me that he came to Port Alberni from the US to do a big construction project and used to go to a little café at 6:00 in the morning. He said my brother Ron came over to his table and said "don't sit by yourself, come over and join our table" and introduced him to all the tug boat guys. He said that he had never met a more gracious man and felt compelled to be at his funeral. Ron was also a great hunter and marksman. When he died I woke up every morning for 2 months feeling like I was late for work and had 2 flat tires.

Mike, Dan and Laura

Mickey & Danny
Being held by Brother Ron

Mickey with his fishing rod

GOING TO SCHOOL
WITH MY SISTER MARJORIE

The next thing I can recall is my sister Marjorie taking me to school at Saint Ann's Convent when I was 5 years old. I was the youngest of a family of 8; 5 boys and 3 girls. I remember we had to walk up rickety old fire escape stairs 3 stories and I was nervous of the heights. I asked Sister Superior about this many years later, as we had a close friendship until her death at age 95, and she said that she always worried about fire and that is why she wanted all the day students and boarders to use the fire escape when entering and leaving the building.

IRENE

One of our boarders was a pretty French Canadian girl who was a student from a nearby town. She always volunteered to clean the blackboard brushes at recess. I saw this as an opportunity to kiss her so I volunteered to stay in class and help her during recess. Well I guess the teacher could see right through my treachery and came back to the class quietly and caught us kissing. I was told to go play outside and she got a huge lecture. Not fair is it? A year later when I was about 15 my brother Dan drove me to her home in Duncan which is about 40 miles from Nanaimo. She knew I was coming and when I got there, on that lovely summer evening, she came out on to the porch looking incredible in a little white top and shorts. Yes, I can still picture her in my mind.

I was being as nice as I knew how when some guys in our car parked about 100' away started saying to me "where for art thou homio?" Without  thinking I turned around and told them to "Fuck Off!" Big mistake as she looked at me with a horrified look and said "I have to go in now". My dreams washed away like the ice in a men's urinal.

BOOTLEGGING AT SCHOOL AND LEGION DANCES

I had a good buddy named Ray who had a gang of his own but one day we got talking and decided that bootlegging booze was a good plan to make money. One day as I was taking piano lessons in a home, the teacher mentioned they had inherited 2 barrels of wine in their basement. Neither she nor her husband drank so one day they would have to get rid of it. My ears perked up and the next time I went I brought 2 one gallon empty jugs and hid them in the alley. After my lesson I went into the basement through an outside door and drained off 2 gallons. Ray and I put them into empty 26oz whiskey bottles and brought them to the next school dance where we were going to sell them to the guys. We charged $2 a bottle, they had to pay upfront and then we would tell him where the bottle was. It was usually "X number of telephone poles north or south of the school", this way we would never get caught handing it over. We did the same thing at the Legion Rock and Roll Dances. The demand grew weekly and we soon drained the 2 barrels.

We were running out of booze so I found this scary looking ex-con who hung around the pool hall. I called him Harry the Mark. He was a scary looking dude about 40 who wore a fedora and a black suit. He had a moustache and the shiftiest eyes that I have ever seen. He agreed to buy all the booze we wanted for 1/3 of the action. This was great! We paid $2.52 per dozen for beer, 90 cents a bottle for berry cup wine and $4.85 for whiskey. We simply charged double and our business expanded to loggers and fisherman after the liquor store was closed. We were doing great until one day Harry got busted for something else and the cops hauled him away. I felt sorry for him as he was always first class with Ray and me. Of course bootlegging has all but died off as off premises sales in bars and longer opening hours came into effect. Ray did not drink and I only had a few drinks with the gang when we used to get together and sing Hank Williams songs

GOOD OLD MILLY

Core members of our gang were
Ron and Gerald Budda.
Their father was
a very crude spoken war
veteran and their mother
was a war bride from
England named Milly.
She had a heart of gold
and may God bless her kind soul. She had been a bar
maid in England and she understood youth. The
father, old Walter, usually worked an afternoon shift
as an orderly at the Indian Hospital. Milly would let
us drink in her kitchen and would make us huge
platefuls of Prem sandwiches. She said I don't care if
you boys drink beer but don't get drunk and drive
your car. She loved it when we sang "Wedding Bells
are Ringing in the Chapel" and old Hank Williams
tunes. There was an old abandoned small house on
the backend of their land where a Chinese man used
to grow vegetables. We made it into our clubhouse
and drank beer and sang every weekend. Pat was a
great artist and he would draw grotesque pictures of
all of us on the walls. We got our beer by phoning a
local taxi company and ordering 6 dozen beers. When
the taxi arrived at Walter's house we would say that
Walter was in the bathtub and he left the money with
us to pay for the beer. We did this week after week.

Fun times with the gang. When I think back, 4 out of
the 9 of us died before the age of 40. One of the guys,
Vic, used to say "I am going to live fast, die young
and leave a good looking corpse". This he did. Miss
you Vic, you were a great guy and friend.

WELFARE IN UNIFORM

The gang decided to join the Canadian Scottish Reserve when we were about 15 or 16, as they met every Thursday night at the local army camp. The great thing about it was we got paid $1.75 for attending and beer was 25 cents a bottle. You could get a fair buzz after the training and maneuvers were over. The training started at 6:30, the bar opened at 8:30, and we would get pissed until 10:30 and be home by 11 pm. In short, it was a great event.

We later had a civil defense course to learn all about the Atomic Bomb. What a crew that was. It consisted of about 50 local misfits, our gang and a few derelict officers. We had a great leader, Sergeant Major Dodds, who was a fine specimen of a Scottish Soldier with a great big waxed moustache, we all loved him. Word was that he was wounded in the Second World War and laid bleeding in a cornfield in Europe, but managed to survive. He had a great sense of humor and he could see no wrong with whatever horseplay we preformed.

I was the second best marksman, only second to Sergeant Bateman, but a young asshole of a corporal did not like the way I held the rifle when I was target shooting. As I was laying down aiming to shoot, he kicked the rifle butt into the side of my face and told me to hold the gun tighter against my face. I kept my cool and asked him to demonstrate. When he was aiming I kicked the gun against his face as hard as I could with my army boots on. His ear was badly cut and he demanded that I be arrested for assaulting an officer. Sergeant Dodds told him, one good demonstration deserves another and laughed in his face. Some of the shit we pulled off in that outfit is best left unprinted. Needless to say that 15 and 16 year old boys should not be carrying around machine guns. Buy me lunch sometime and I will tell you some wild stories. God bless Sergeant Major Dodds and I salute you.

P.S. One day another idiot officer took it upon himself to check out all of our birth certificates in Victoria as the lame brain suspected a large group of us were underage. He found out that about 20 of the 50 of us were not 18 as required by law. When Dodds found out he went ballistic and had everyone stand at attention on the parade square. He berated the officer who caused our dismissal mercilessly for a good 5 minutes calling him every kind of backstabbing rat he could think of. He ended his tirade with "if I had my way you would be shot and pissed on". Well, that ended my military career.

GOOD OLD ERIC

One day when I was about 13 I was riding my bike down a back alley and I discovered a great patch of blackberries in the back yard of an old dilapidated house 2 blocks from my home. I knocked on the door and an old man with one eye and very few teeth answered. When I say he had one eye I mean that his missing eye was just a white hollow. He told me that I could pick all the blackberries I wanted anytime. I went home and got my bucket and when I was finished he gave me a large bunch of the most beautiful gladiolas for my mother. This began a close relationship with old Eric and me. His name was Eric John May and was born in England. He was what they called a remittance man, which means his family (his father was a clergyman) did not really want him around so they sent him to Canada when he was a young man where he received a modest sum of money sent to him every month.

He joined the Canadian Army in 1914 and was sent to Europe where he became a veteran of the famous "Vimy Ridge Tunnel Attack". He told me dozens of stories about the war. He told me that once they reached a farm house in France, after weeks in the trenches, they would borrow a hot iron off of the top of a woodstove and press their clothes and you could hear the crab lice popping like popcorn. They used diesel oil on their bodies to get rid of crab lice or at least keep them down to a dull roar. He lost his eye in a logging accident here on Vancouver Island. He was also badly mauled by a huge dog that tore up his face. He would let me and a few friends come into his house at night where he always had a big round loaf of bread in a drawer and we could put peanut butter and jam on the thick pieces of bread cut from the enormous loaf. A big pot of tea washed it all down. In my mind I can still see the patterned bread board and the knife.

Eric had lived through tough times and had hundreds of cans of food under his bed. Over the next few years more boys started to come to Eric's house. I threw out anybody I did not like and when I say threw out I mean I threw them over the top rail of his front porch into the blackberry vines if they did not leave voluntarily.

Every once in a while Eric would get us to weed his garden and give us some money to go over to the Nova Store for chocolate bars. One day when I was 15, I asked him if I could clean out an old room that he never used so that I could entertain my girlfriend Sally in privacy. He told me that I could so I cleaned out what little there was in there and put it in the basement. I painted the walls and the wooden floor and put a blue light bulb in the ceiling. Eric bought a new couch and I was in business. I remember Sally's Mother phoning my Mother concerned that we were spending too much time together and my Mother telling her that she could not speak for her daughter but her son would only be interested in study. Aren't Moms great?

Some years later I was selling Christmas trees in Vancouver and when I came home I went to visit Eric. The neighbor Jack told me that he had slipped on his stairway and had fractured his ankle and was in the veteran's hospital in Vancouver. I phoned and they told me he had died of pneumonia. I used to say to him "you are a good guy Eric" as he sat in his old leather lined rocking chair with his right hand covering the spot where his eye was missing and he would say "some say good old Eric and some say fuck old Eric". I say "good old Eric".

SWEET MARIE

I was going out with a perky little gal named Patsy and one day I told her to find a girlfriend for my friend Don as he was not much of a shaker and a mover. I told her that if she could find a date for Don, we could get Don's father's car, a hard top Olds, and go to the drive-in. She said she knew a very shy girl who might want to go. She lined up a girl named Marie and off we went to the drive-in. She was a girl of Russian extraction who had raven black hair and very white skin. She was very polite and had a good sense of humour. I went to her house the next day and asked her to be my girlfriend and she said she would. I was absolutely nuts about her and she was a beauty. Her mother hated me but her father liked me.

We were together for about 2 years and I wanted to marry her. The problem was that I had no job and very little money. I told her I was going to go up to the interior of the province to find a job and get the funds to marry her. She told me if I went with my buddy Pat (Wino) that she would leave me, she hated him because he used to tease her all the time and she was very sensitive, but I went anyway as there was no work around Nanaimo at this time.

We ended up in Castlegar, only to find out that because of the very wet spring, the river was too high to start any construction on the proposed dams that were to be built in that area.

We took a job logging with this haywire outfit and we bunked in a cabin with no mattress or covers. All we had to eat was a pot of spaghetti that we warmed up in the morning on an old stove. By the third morning the spaghetti had maggots churning around in the pot. We asked the boss to bring us some food or an advance to buy some grub. The bastard refused so we quit with no pay and headed back the 35 miles to Castlegar. We had 10 days left on our $40 per month apartment and 20 cents in cash, plus the gas we siphoned out of any car or truck that we could get close to. I remember one night we were siphoning gas out of this guy's Mercury van when low and behold he was sleeping in it. It surprised the hell out of him, and us, and we took off with our hose and his gas. We decided to spend our last 20 cents (the price of beer at that time) on a glass of beer at the Marlane Hotel. The bartenders name was Wolfgang and we told him that was our last 20 cents. He told us to go to the local pulp mill as they were hiring workers to refractor the mill. We gulped down our beer along with one that Wolfgang gave us, and to our delight we were hired on the spot.

We worked 12 hour shifts 8pm till 8am. One night we had to crawl through a long pipe into a gas furnace and stand on a scaffold and jack hammer brick away from the steel, it was hot as hell in there and we sweated like crazy. A few days later we packed bricks into a lime kiln and that was heavy work. But a few nights we just sat on the steel grated stairway and waited to be told what to do next. One night I told the foreman that I was afraid that I would get fired for just sitting there but he told me not to rock the boat as it was all cost plus. After 2 weeks we got paid what we considered to be a fortune. We did not realize that the company we were working for was a union company and that the last 4 hours of our 12 hour shift was double time. Sundays and holidays were triple time. We could not believe the sum of our checks so we went to the bank and cashed them, figuring that they had made a big mistake and we took off out of town.

Talk about Mutt and Jeff. Loaded, we headed to a new area. We got to a little town named Applevale and were driving down a country road in my 51 Monarch hard top when I saw a pretty girl trying to herd some cows into a corral. She had bare feet and they were covered in cow dung, but she was a beauty. Polly was her name. I got out of my car and without talking, I ran to the back of the herd and together we got all the cows into the corral. She thanked me and asked me where I was from. She told me that she and her sister were being beaten by her father and brother, they had no rights and were planning to run away from the abuse. We told them "if you want to leave we can meet here at midnight and take off to the coast". They were ready and away we went. We were flushed with cash so we drove until about 5pm and then rented a motel room where we stayed for about 3 days. Polly told me that she had phoned a girlfriend back in Applevale and was told that her father had said she had been kidnapped and the police were looking for her. The next morning when Wino and I woke up the girls were gone. They left a note saying they did not want us to go to jail for helping them escape so they were going back to say they had run away. I was devastated, but as Tony Soprano would say "What are you gonna do?" So Wino and I headed back to Nanaimo.

When I got back I phoned my girlfriend Marie. She told me a cousin of hers in Castlegar had told her that I had a girlfriend the whole time I was working there.

She believed her cousin and didn't want to see me. I thought "what the hell" the whole reason I went to Castlegar was to get some money together so I could marry her!

A week later Wino and I got a good skin full of beer at the old Lotus Hotel and I got pining away for Marie. I decided to go to her house at 11pm even though I was pissed. I knew her father, who was a carpenter, and he had a long ladder behind the house. I got Wino to help me put the ladder up against the ledge of her window upstairs. I climbed up the ladder and tapped on her window and she came to the window. We were reconciling pretty good when her mother showed up in the dark with a big mop and knocked me off of the top of the ladder. I landed right on top of poor Wino and we both got the wind knocked out of us. We lay on the ground moaning and groaning.

Marie's mom had phoned the cops who were stationed only 3 blocks away so they got there in minutes. We were still on the ground when they got there. They started laughing and could not stop. When we finally got our breath back they said "you two piss tank hillbillies had better get into your car and get back up on the mountain or we will run you in". A tragic thing happened to Marie a few years later when on her honeymoon, she and her husband were in an accident and he was killed. I went to visit her when she was in the local hospital in serious condition and there was Big Mama who put the run on me once again. A love unfinished is a profound desire unfulfilled.

MY UNCLE GEORGE GIVING ME 50 CENTS

One day my father's half-brother George Metro came to visit my father. George lived in San Francisco. He went to the USA after the violent strikes in the coal mines here on Vancouver Island. He gave me 50 cents and I was so happy about it. There is an interesting story about George. It is said that when the strikes were on in the mines, he was thrown off the train by its employees because he was a striker. He came back to Ladysmith many years later and tracked the men down and kicked the shit out of them then quickly returned to San Francisco where he was a

manager of the cable cars. He was a good looking man who dressed up like Colonel Saunders, rings and all, and was a dedicated ladies' man in his older years after his wife had passed away. One day I was working in the field and to my surprise I saw Uncle George walking in the field on our farm. I was surprised and hollered "Uncle George is that you?" At the time he was in his eighties. He told me he had to come see the cabin and field that he was raised on. I told him he must come to my house and stay with us, but he politely said no and just walked away into the field. He returned home to San

Francisco and died shortly after when a main artery ruptured, as a result of an injury from an old mining accident.

George loved to work with cement and when he came to visit he always built sidewalks or whatever. On a hot day he would say to me as a boy, "Mickey, do you have any lemonade?" and I would say "no but there is a cold beer" and he would say "drinking beer will ruin your kidneys but if that is what you got then I will have one". His Favorite saying was "Nothing is too dirty for a Republican".

MY BROTHER EDDY
BEATING UP TWO BOYS

Another memory of my boyhood is one day when my brother Danny and I were playing outside in the yard and some older boys walked by on the street. For some reason they started giving us a hard time and threatened to kick our asses. Within minutes, my older brother Eddy, came running out of the house and onto the street to give them a terrible and bloody beating. It scared me. I actually felt sorry for those poor bastards.

Ed Gogo, Sister Superior and Mike

SISTER SUPERIOR
AND THE PHONE CALL TO MY HOME

I always got into a lot of trouble at school, something about not listening. So one day I was sent to the office for some misbehaviour. It must have been serious as Sister Superior made me phone my mother and tell her what I had done. I thought I could pull off an academy performance and pretend I was talking to my mother. I thought I had pulled it off until I was ending the call when she said "Mickey let me talk to your mother". Oh oh! Now I remember the offence was, I had carved a whale on the top of my wooden desk... So much for art.

Pretty Betty

KISSING BETTY THROUGH THE FLYSCREEN

There was a very cute little gal by the name of Betty and I was attracted to her like a magnet. But how could a boy of 14 make a move on her in a convent school? I gave this as much thought as a man trying to break out of jail, only I was trying to break in to see Betty. I came up with the idea of cutting a hole in the fly screen so I cold kiss her but there was never any opportunity for privacy. Foiled once again! We remain lifelong friends to this day.

LITTLE ANTHONY AND THE FLOOR WAX

I attended the convent school for 8 years and my best friend was little Anthony Bortolotto. He had sideburns and a thick goatee by the time he was 12. Although he played goal in hockey he was the best skater I had ever seen. He could stop the puck and away he would go down the ice and pass it to a team member. Because the coaches got on his case, he quit playing, which was a shame. He was the most mischievous boy, and one day as a nun was walking up the stairs he tried to lift her long skirt up from behind. Unfortunately another nun saw him and we were both busted. I was near him and guilt by association ruled that day. Our punishment was to de-wax and re-wax a very long hallway.

PUKING IN CHURCH

Can anything be more embarrassing than upchucking in church? I remember a Wednesday when I was in church and not feeling well. I thought I might get in trouble if I left during the service. I continued to feel worse and as I got up from a kneeling position I suddenly ralphed right on the neck of a poor kid in front of me. I thought I was going to get shot for the performance, but a nun took me outside to the garden, washed me down with a garden hose and sympathized with me. After hurling and not getting shot I felt much better.

BIG EDDY GALANT

One day while playing soccer at school a lad named Big Eddy tried to kick the soccer ball in mid air. He missed and kicked me right on my dink. It didn't hurt that much but it turned all kinds of colours over the next week, including candy apple burgundy. That same year my buddy Lenny sat on my bike to double ride with me and crushed my poor stem-winder. It reminded me of that Frank Sinatra song "It Was a Very Good Year" only for my poor jewel it was a very bad year. I used to go to a little café called the IXL with Eddy's brother Bernie where you could get a milkshake and hamburger for 35 cents.

THE JOYS OF FARTING ON YOUR BROTHER

We three youngest brothers all slept in one big bed and two of us were known to be less than fragrant, so we put the un-gassy one in between us at night and we would put our bums up against him and give him a good number of cannonading blasts. He would get so mad at us but what could the poor guy do about it?

MY SAFE & STRUCTURED CHILDHOOD

My father had a huge yard that covered the whole block and at the other end there was a small house that he rented out to an old retired farmer from Saskatchewan. We had apple trees, cherry trees, pear trees, and every kind of berry bush known to man. We lived in a house that was a bit crowded but never dirty, as my mother Phyllis was scrupulously clean and made sure the rest of the herd was as well. She was an unbelievably hard worker. She got up at 5 a.m., made a big breakfast for my father and older brothers then the younger ones as well as packed our lunches. There was always a big supper with plenty for all including great pies and such. At about 8:00 p.m. she would be putting fresh bread in the oven for the next day. Sunday meant going to mass and I can tell you "no mass", "no eat." Often, her older brother Rolly would come over mid Sunday afternoon with a fresh steelhead salmon that he had caught that morning at the Nanaimo River Falls. Supper was always followed by watching Ed Sullivan on TV and lemon pie for dessert.

During her final days she had heart trouble and was in hospital and I knew she was not coming out. As I drove along I would think "your mother is in the hospital dying you asshole, why are you not going there to visit her right now?" I would change direction and go straight to see her. She told me at the end that because of the side-effects of the medicines she had to take, she had no quality of life. The day she died, I drove to the farm to tell my father and asked him if he wanted a drink but he declined and said "I will deal with my sorrow in my way and in my time". He explained to me that the person who is gone feels no pain or sorrow but the survivors do. They were married 49 years, had eight children and 37 grandchildren. When they lowered her coffin in the grave, I noticed a singular tear run down my father's face. In my opinion, she was a saint. Whenever I help out a nephew or niece and they would ask me why, I would say, Mother would have wanted it that way. She was the boss.

TOMBOLA TICKETS

We used to sell raffle tickets called Tombola for the school and I used to go through our unique ethnic neighbourhood called Five Acres but now called Harewood. We had a Swedish family, the Andersons; a French family, the Ouimets; a Welsh family, the Merosolaves and on and on. No two the same. But I can't remember any significant problems. Anyway, one day I went to the house of this old bachelor fisherman from Croatia. When I knocked on the door I was told to come in and sit down. The Fisherman asked me what I wanted. When I told him, his drinking partner, a man named Ben, called me a superstitious little bastard of a Catholic. I was a little afraid but the Fisherman asked me how many books of tickets I had and I told him 3 books with 12 tickets to the book. They were 10 cents each or 3 for 25 cents and the prize was always an Indian sweater knitted and donated by our First Nation parishioners.

The fisherman said, I will buy all 3 and you ride your bike back to the convent and get 10 more right now, then I will buy them as well. This really pissed off his buddy Ben to no end and the fisherman just laughed at him and was true to his word.

BEAUTIFUL ROMANO BORTOLOTTO

Remember my wild little friend Anthony? Well he was an only child and his father was a logger. His father, Romano, was always impeccably dressed. Even his caulk boots and raingear were packaged military correct when he came home from the woods. He used to be one of the men who passed around the collection at church, along with a big old man name Nick who owned the local pool hall. Romano was so well dressed and always had the perfect pencil line moustache. He was so kind and polite to everyone. I remember taking my son David to Romano's home when David was 1 year old. Romano was so happy. I loved him.

FATHER HANLY AND THE CROSS

One day we were playing baseball at lunch time and Father Hanly came over from the rectory to the convent for lunch. He stopped and said "May I have a turn at bat?" He hit the ball so far up in the air he actually knocked one of the side arms off of the cross on the top of the church, really an incredible feat. We were all shocked that anyone could do that but he laughed and said "Don't tell Monseigneur or we will all be in trouble, say it must have been lightning."

When you got into "Big Trouble" you had to go see Father Hanly but he was never judgmental and you always left his office feeling better about yourself. In spite of the fact that per capita the Catholic Church has less reports of pedophilia than any other denomination, they seem to get all the bad publicity. I remember one time Father Ratchford told all of us alter boys that if anyone, clergy or otherwise, tried to molest us we were to go to the police station next door to the school or tell our parents or an older brother.

CHRIS THE BULLY

There was a kid at the convent that was really mean and evil. He was an older boy and made school miserable for the smaller boys. He was cunning and sneaky and always picked his spots of abuse so that there were no witnesses. When he was 18 he was killed in a car accident. Karma?

HUMMING BIRDS

Think about the most amazing thing that you have ever seen. To me it is the hummingbird. If you had never seen one and somebody told you that there is a bird that can stop in the air and fly backwards no one would believe it. We take the miracles of nature for granted.

WHATEVER HAPPENED TO LENNIE DAGALIEZ?

One of my good buddies at the convent was Lenny Dagaliez. He was a German boy with an older brother named Henry who was extremely intelligent in all subjects at school. There was a terrible accident and Lennie's father was killed in a logging accident. I remember Lennie's mother crying for weeks and it was too sad. Lenny and I took off and played hooky for a week. We would climb up trees and sometimes hang upside down like monkeys. Sister Superior never gave us hell for it and told me a year later that it was because I kept Lennie's mind off his sorrows for a little while.

STEALING BANANAS FROM THE DUTCHMAN

There was a ruddy faced Dutchman name Jack Kokshorn who had an old Mercury van filled with fruit and vegetables. He would go door to door and sell the housewives his product. He was an incredibly hard worker as most Dutch people are. When he would go into our house to sell my mother vegetables, my brother Dan and I would quickly sneak into his van and steal some bananas. One day many years later I was talking about this at the lunch table and said I regretted stealing from this poor man. My father spoke up and said "don't feel too sorry because he told me what you were up to and I told him to just add it to our bill." Old pops said as long as we were eating them he didn't care.

THE MUSIC TEACHER
AND THE THIEVING ALTER BOY

We had a wonderful music and dancing teacher, a lady teacher named June. She encouraged me to learn to sing and dance and she put on countless concerts for the parish.   All students were included.   I remember my role in a singing story of candies as I was dressed up as Mr.Coughdrop. I can still recall my singing part verbatim. On another note I caught an alter boy stealing from the parish collection after Sunday mass and I promptly turned him in. I was no angel but that act disgusted me and made me angry. I would have liked to kick the shit out of him but others in his family were great kids so I did not want to start a family feud.
All of these activities were looked over by Monsignor

Baker, a dedicated man from Quebec who was probably the best front man the parish of Nanaimo has ever known.

He took on the challenge of building a huge new church and ran an unbelievably successful church bingo where about 75% of the money went back to the players. A local postman, Mr. Jack Sherry, played a huge roll in paying off the church. Jack also was a tireless force behind senior lacrosse in Nanaimo. It became the talk of the town and even the police got involved because of pressure from the other bingos in the community. Monseigneur recognized two RCMP plain clothes officers and promptly threw them out of the hall. He once told the parish that the good news was that there was enough money in the parish to build a new church the bad news was that it was still in the parishioners' pockets. When they had his funeral, they put his big purple hat on top of the coffin and I cried, God Rest and God Bless Monseigneur Baker.

COULD BUY IT AT
THE CONVENT FOR 5 CENTS

My father was the owner of a lot of land and employed many people and certainly paid his fair share of taxes including school tax, but none of his 8 children ever went to a public school except myself and I only went there for grades nine and ten. We all went to private school and of course he paid for that as well. In Ontario or Quebec, parents can pay their school taxes directly to the private school they attend but the politicians here at that time were mostly a group of old wasp types so us Catholics were not represented fairly. As Catholics, we were not allowed to ride the school bus, so I can relate to people who are discriminated against. I got in trouble for not wearing my school uniform but did this so I could get home without walking.

There was a big bully that I called Lardhead and he would tell the bus driver that I should not be allowed on the bus as I was a convent kid, as we were called. Unfortunately for me, we got off at the same stop and he would rough me up. I soon tired of this, so one day I put a nice sized rock in my pocket and when I got off the bus after him he was waiting for me with a big ugly grin on his face. I took the rock out of my pocket and had it in my right hand so when I came down the stairs off the bus, I threw the rock into his face as hard as I could. Blood galore! But he left me alone after that.

So this concludes my convent years except to mention our Mayor, Pete Maffeo. Never enough good things could ever be said about Pete. He was most generous with children and sports teams of all stripes. He owned an ice plant and also manufactured ice-cream bars in many flavours. Often he would send a case of these to the convent as his plant was only 2 blocks away. He always said that he had to get it out of his plant as his refrigerator had broken down but we all knew better. He would bring the Harlem Globetrotters to Nanaimo and feed them all right out of his house. His memory is legend.

One last convent story: When I was about 14, I served mass in the Nun's Chapel every morning at 6:00 a.m. during my summer holidays. I used to boost flowers for the alter on the way to serve mass. I got too carried away so a nun told me to slack off as she doubted that there were that many high quality flowers on vacant lots.

I have polled many kids I went to the convent school with and almost all of the boys thought it was great but most all of the girls resented it. So why is that? I think the nuns catered more to the boys because in the day the boys were going to be something, as they used to call it and the girls, not so much. Realistically the only thing the girls could aspire to was to become a secretary or a nurse. The girls resented this but that was the way it was back then. I tell the girls now that is unfair of them to judge the sisters with 2013 standards for what transpired in 1955. Just sayin…..

THE TINY NUN SAYING "YOU'RE THE BAD ONE"

There was an elderly and very tiny nun that as far as I could tell had no position. I figure she was just old and nobody wanted to see her go to a retirement home. Anyhow, she used to say to me every day in a crackling voice "you come from a good family but you're the bad one aren't you?" and then she would laugh. I took no offence as she was a little sweetie.

STEALING IS OUR ALLOWANCE

When I was a kid no one ever heard of an allowance so when we wanted money we had to get it ourselves. I did this by teaming up with my neighbourhood buddy, Carl, and we would go out at night and steal batteries out of cars. Not in our neighbourhood of course, but not too far away as we had to pack these heavy suckers up near the old junkyard and hide them in the bush until things died down and then we would sell them to old Adrian, a Jew who had a junkyard, no questions asked. Another partner in crime was my good pal Albino. We used to go out at night and steal 1 chicken each night so it wouldn't be missed and we would put them in a shed behind his house. We fed them with grain that we swept from empty grain cars at the farmer's co-op. On Saturday, we would take them to an old Italian lady who made and sold chicken tamales and she paid us 50 cents a bird. Needless to say, no question asked.

NOBODY HAS 8 KIDS!

When I was about 13 I asked my father what it is like to have 8 kids and he told me no one has 8 kids, so I replied, "you do." He told me that a couple has 1 and then 1 more and if everyone is healthy and happy then it becomes a big family, so I guess that is the way he saw it. It is a fact that I never heard my father swear or give bad example. One day, when I was a little boy, my father hired a man who had a huge pair of plough horses and I remember the man's hat had about an inch of dust on it. After he had finished the ploughing, my father paid him and they started discussing large logging corporations. The man did not like a certain company and let fly describing them with a mile long string of profanity, the likes of which to this day, I never witnessed. My poor dad put his hands over my ears but I heard it all. My dad was just the greatest guy and the day of my first marriage, I noticed him going outside the building at the reception. It seemed strange, so I went outside and asked him if he was okay. He seemed sad and told me that when I was a young boy, I harassed him to buy me a fancy bike like my friend Gregory had and he always felt bad that at the time we couldn't afford it as he had been sick for a while with no money coming in. I felt terrible and told him that I considered myself a spoiled boy and told him that he was always the best father a guy could have. I hope he believed me.

How I did get a bike was as follows: My good friend, Gregory had a father who was a dentist and Gregory was an only child. His dad consumed alcohol day and night and was extremely coarse in his language. One day, Greg asked him for a new bike and his dad, Duncan, looked at me and said, Gogo, do you have a new bike and I told him "no sir, I do not have any bike." So he called Greg, a spoiled little prick as that is how he talked. He told Greg that if he wanted to get a new bike, he had to give me his old bike and so we both ended up happy.

Old Duncan used to take Gregory and me out on his yacht fishing and he always brought along a 22 rifle. He told Greg, who was a great little guy but a city boy, to shoot some seagulls but Greg was a kind boy and he declined. His father called him a wimp and said "Gogo, do you want to pop off a few shit hawks?" I so wanted to shoot those gulls but said no as Duncan had really put me in a bind. Poor Greg. Greg became a tennis pro but died very young of stomach cancer. He was a warm and fuzzy little pal.

1st row 5th person – Maureen Horrocks
1st row 6th person – Shirley Gannon
2nd row 1st person – Greg Fox
2nd row 4th person – Lenny Daga1ise
2nd row last person – Tony Bortolotto
3rd row 1st person – David Campell
3rd row 3rd person – Dan Gogo
3rd row 4th person – Ronnie Gannon
3rd row 5th person – Mickey Gogo
3rd row 6th person – Al Bassanello

Al (Bass) Basanello

PRETTY LITTLE SHIRLEY

There were two families with the most beautiful Irish girls and they were cousins. There were about 7 girls in total. It would be hard to say who was the prettiest, but Shirley would be a top contender. When I was about 12 all I could think of was running away with her to a mountain cabin and I did not even know why. She recently passed away and to my great disappointment, she requested no funeral take place. I feel strongly that a person from a large family should have a funeral, so that the family can appreciate the love and memory for the departed, otherwise what was that all about ? I have noticed that at recent funerals some appoint a spokesperson and others are not afforded a chance to speak. In my opinion if people are in that big of a hurry they should not attend.

SISTER SUPERIOR

At the convent we had a Sister Superior.
I always loved that title. In my case, she was superior to any person that I ever met. Once in a while she would come out and play soccer, baseball

and badminton with the students. She was proficient with all that she did including running a big school and staff. Even long after retirement she did advocacy work for many people that fell through the bureaucratic cracks in our society. I know of many lives enriched by her tireless efforts. I kept in touch over the years and she loved going with me to a "Dim Sum" lunch in Victoria's Chinatown. She died at the age of 95. I visited her in the hospital and sat beside her bed. She was cheerful as ever, but I broke down crying and she ended up comforting me. I finally got it together and said to her "you know that you have a reservation in heaven don't you?" she smiled and nodded.

HOW TO CREATE A BOMB "THE BASANELLOS"

You remember my old chicken stealing partner Albino? Well this was the result of an explosive pairing of an Irish mother and an Italian father. They had 3 children, Albino and his two younger pretty sisters, Cathleen and Irene. I used to wrestle Bass, as I called him, all the time and we had a rule that the first guy to throw the other to the ground would win the round. One night we were wrestling on the grass on a late spring evening outside of Old Erics house and as he came toward me he slipped on the grass and broke his leg. He was in great pain and I said we have to phone an ambulance but he didn't want to because his mother would kill him. She was like a volcano and had a most violent temper. I remember a time when she had a big row with her husband. I felt sorry for him as he loved his children and was a hardworking man. She threw him out of the house with a hell of a performance as she keep ranting on and on.

A young priest came to the house with a bowl of ice cream and gave it to the kids out on the back porch and went in the house to try and settle her down. That's the way things were in those days. I don't think the young priest could do anything that would calm her on an ongoing basis, so they divorced. I remember Albino's dad meeting the kids on the corner bringing them gifts. He was a good man and he and his children deserved better.

Cathleen and I were boyfriend and girlfriend at one time but she dumped me and I went out with her younger sister Irene. Cathy got mad and said to her sister "you're not going out with that guy are you?" to which Irene replied "why not? You did." When I say going out together I mean holding hands and maybe the rare little kiss. Innocence abounded in those days.

MR. CARL ANDERSON

My Swedish friend Carl lived alone with his father. His father was a master boat builder and always had a project going in his garage. I remember one day picking some blackberries and giving them to him.

The next day he told his son Carl to bring me in the house and he served me all the delicious blackberry pie and ice cream I could eat. It was the best blackberry pie ever.

LOUIS TOGNELLO

When I was a boy my mother used to send me to Tognello's farm to buy eggs. They were 50 cents a dozen and my mom would put a 2$ bill in the bottom of my bucket and away I would go walking about a half a mile to their basement where they candled the eggs. In the basement there was a chair and a candle but also a huge wooden barrel of red wine and about 25 of the biggest salamis I have ever seen. They were about 3 inches wide and 3 feet long. Mrs. Tognello, Rosa was a most pleasant lady who always had a smile for me and most everyone else. Every so often she would be busy making supper or something and her husband Louis would come down to candle the eggs. He was a huge man and smoked a huge pipe. He would sit down, take a big tin cup off a nail that was on a supporting post and drain off a cup of wine.

He would then take a knife and cut a thick piece off one of the big salamis. It took him about one hour to get me 4 dozen eggs. One day I looked at him with astonishment at his unbridled consumption, he caught me looking and said with a strong Italian accent "I drinka the wine boy, I drinka the wine" and I thought no shit Louie. A parting thought…they had an apple tree that grew huge apples that they gave me to take home to my mother. She would take the core out, fill the hole with brown sugar and raisins and a splash of rum and bake them in the oven, delicious.

KILLING THE GOAT

I knew this lady name Mrs. Young who told me she liked goat meat so I bought a young goat at a cattle auction and brought it home. I knew nothing about how to care for it so my poor dad got stuck raising it. I remember when he slaughtered it as it was not a pleasant thing for a young boy to watch. One goat sale was enough for me.

When I was 13 I used to sell salami pigs for Pop Hawkins. We charged 13 cents a pound, delivered after slaughter and my commission was 1 cent a pound. I sold a lot of them as I knew all the Italians because I used to sell the tombola tickets from the convent to them. It was easy money for me as when one Italian got his pig he would always tell me the name of another Italian who wanted to buy one. They preferred boars to sows, the bigger the better. I made good money for a kid and it taught me how to sell and deal with ethnic folks.

HOW TO MAKE IT PAY CUTTING HAY

When I was 14 my dad had a little McCormick Farmall Cub Tractor that was equipped to cut and rake hay. The going rate at the time was $7 per hour that included the driver and the tractor. Many of our neighbors had 5 acre parcels of land, in fact, what is now Harewood was called Five Acres. In the day the mining company sold 5 acre blocks to employees and most folks had a cow, chickens and a good sized garden. I would ride my bike to the neighbors and give them a price to cut and rake their fields. Most fields had huge crops as they loaded the fields with chicken manure in the fall, man that stuff stinks!!! By late May the grass grew so tall that the winds knocked it over always in one direction. If you cut from the wrong side you would waste a lot of hay but if you cut into it you would get it as close to the ground as a shave. So I would give them a price of say $90 but it would only take me 8 hours to cut it. So when I got home my dad said I could take a cut of the $7 per hour but I told him no and gave him $56 with the balance for me. The neighbors were always happy with my work and the big yield from cutting it right. As old Pop Hawkins would say "Mickey!!! you don't get what you deserve you get what you negotiate." One year we cut the big Westwood Farm fields and we cut all day and all night in the moonlight as deer gazed in the distance. One day I was bailing hay and I stopped the tractor to tighten the bailer string tying levers. Like a fool I did not lower my bucket and the vamping of the bailer started the machine rolling down the hill toward a creek. I was very afraid that I would get run over by the tractor and then the bailer but the little tractor and bailer were all we had so I ran alongside of the tractor and managed to hang on to the steering wheel and hop on the seat. Thank you Jesus. With that tractor we pulled out small logs, cut hay, racked hay, pulled carts and trailers of Christmas trees and hoisted slaughtered cattle hauled away the offal and buried it. It is still around over at my brother Dan's.

TARZAN

I went to the convent school with a guy named Chris Balatti who was a nice quiet boy naturally built like Tarzan. I would go to his boxing fights and cheer him on. He would box a round or two then he would wink at me and throw a hard stiff jab at his opponent. When the man he was boxing against put his gloves up to cover his eyes he would nail them with a vicious overhand right to the solar plexus. Bam!!! He would put them on the canvas and they did not get up for a long time. He could have gone a long way but he marched to a different drum.

THE BROPHY'S

When I was a kid about 13 and attended St. Ann's Convent I used to hang with a guy named Bob Brophy who was a cool guy. He was sort of a beatnik, funny and different. I used to call him "the professor" because he looked scholarly and mature. He had wonderful parents that actually treated young teenagers like human beings. It was the first time that

I had ever met parents that tried to communicate with their children and their children's friends. Bob also had a younger sister Diane who was very attractive and had a dynamite personality. When George Bush Senior invaded Iraq about 700 people in our town staged a peace rally and there were a good number of veterans in uniform in our march. Mr. Brophy Sr. was there and wearing his military uniform and I was marching near him. As we were marching a punk in a pick up truck kept driving by and yelling out at us "You chicken shit bastards" I was livid as I thought of all the brave veterans in our march and how they had to endure this loud mouth punk. Just then an RCMP officer stopped the traffic so we could cross Fitzwilliam Street safely. I noticed the punk was stuck in the traffic so I walked up to his truck and slugged him right in his face as he was still cursing at the marchers. There was a police man only about 30 feet away so the punk said to the cop "arrest him, you saw what he did to me" and the cop told him that he was lucky that all the demonstrators did not drag him out of his truck and kick the shit out of him. Bob gave me shit and told me I was hurting the cause. I did not agree but respected his opinion. God bless Ma and Pa Brophy.

LOOSING MY VIRGINITY

A group of us teenagers used to hang around together and listen to records and do a little dancing. There were these two sisters whose parents were, at that time quite liberated and let a bunch of us hang around their house. The older of the 2 sisters was very busty and extroverted and the other was petite and more reserved. One night the older one, we shall call her Sharon volunteered to walk me halfway home which would be in the middle of the old Chinatown. We stopped under the eves of the old school house and it was just getting dark. I actually felt wimpy having a girl walk me home and little did I know the price I would pay. She told me that she liked me and started kissing me, no resistance from me and it progressed to the point that she undid her brassiere and 20 minutes later I was wound up like an 8 day clock. She told me to meet her at the same place the next night and she would allow the big event to happen. You can imagine my little addled teenage brain that night. So we met the following day at 6pm and we walked to a large wooded acreage a few blocks from the school. It was a late spring day and we walked until we found a secluded grassy knoll and nature took its course. It was wonderful. About 3 days later she told me she was pregnant and I was mortified. She told me not to worry as she had a steady boyfriend who would marry her. Well I kept close tabs on her as I knew who her boyfriend was. I worried my butt off for 8 months until a girl named Joan asked me why I looked so worried. I confided in her and she told me I was being put on and all I had to do is look at the girl and see that she was not pregnant. What a relief but I don't think that I have ever trusted a woman since.

THE GOOD LAWYER

When I was about 16 I was to appear once again in front of the old hanging judge we called "Potsy". A lawyer pulled me aside and told me not to appear in front of him because he knew that "Potsy" would throw me into the slammer. He said he would represent me at no charge and rearranged my court date so that I would appear in front of a different judge. He got me acquitted so you gotta love that.

A little footnote: Just last weekend a man was sitting at a table next to me at a dinner theatre in Victoria and I will be damned if it was not him. It had been 47 years since I had seen him but something told me I knew him. Sure enough when I confronted him it was the good lawyer. He was, as usual, very gracious and I thanked him again.

STEALING COINS FROM THE JAM CAN

My oldest brother worked out of town for Nanaimo Bulldozing and he used to put all of his loose change in an old jam can he had in one of his dresser drawers. One day my brother Dan and I discovered his treasure and we took a 25 cent coin or 2 bits as it was known then and went down to this tiny little corner store called Janies. With 25 cents we each got a pop, 7 cents a bottle at that time, and the rest we spent on candy called jaw breakers that cost 3 for a penny. The can was about ¾ full but after innumerous pilfering you could now see the bottom of the can, so we laid off. He came home one weekend and discovered the loss. We were about 10 years old at the time. He knew it was me and came chasing after me and I ran to get to the bathroom, lock the door and escape out of the window. He was too fast and he caught me and was trying to flush me down the toilet but Dad heard the commotion and told him to put me down. He would not listen so Pops cuffed him and sent him tumbling into the bathtub and he was out cold. My mother was angry at my dad, but once again I cannot remember getting any real punishment for doing it.

THE BIG CHANGE

The school that I went to for the first 8 years was Saint Ann's Convent. It used to teach grades 1 to 13 (13 being university entrance). When I was in grade 8 the Convent changed, after all those years, to teach grades 1 to 8 only. I hope it was not to get rid of me. Grade 9 was my first year in public school and it was another world to me. At the convent one nun taught all the subjects and when she thought we were half asleep she would get out a soccer ball and we would charge outside for a 20 minute game or until oxygen was once again flowing to our brains. There were no combination locks, no lockers, no moving from room to room. I was totally lost in public school but a very pretty girl with a huge personality took pity on me and helped me with combination locks. I had never seen one before. How do you get to all the different rooms? The girl was very kind and very pretty, she still is. Thank you Robin.

Of course the school bullies thought that I would be an easy boy to fight with, but that was not the case as I had always boxed and I had plenty of street fights under my belt. I was also aggressive as I felt it was best to strike first when a fight was inevitable. I had trouble when a group of them tried to get me where no one could see what they were up to. No one wanted to get the shit beat out of them in front of their peers so they did not push it too far. I really lucked out when Ken Stewart, who was a very good hockey goal tender (in those days they played without masks) and Arty, a guy who just got out of reform school, arrived at our school. Water found its own level that day and we became a hell raising threesome. Ken had a car, actually a panel delivery. Remember this was grade 9, so no one had their own car except Ken and I. Mine was a Model A that had no license plates or insurance (See Old School Cover) but the principal told me I could bring it to school as long as I did not park it on school land. The principal's name was Harry Martin, a first class old war vet and one of the few who sympathized with my plight of school changes. Our threesome used to get into Ken's panel and go up to the Harwood Bluffs and drink some wine with our lunch. Soon the word got around that we were having a few swallows at lunch so a lady teacher took it upon herself to tell the girls in her class to stay away from us as we were bad news. Of course you know what happened, a pile of the more adventurous girls joined us for lunch. As Frank Sinatra would sing "it was a very good year".

Robin

I had a homeroom teacher we called "Moose", he was a big man with a brush cut, and I suspect that most mornings he was hung over. He warned us constantly that if we got caught talking in class he would personally strap us. By the way there was no strapping at the convent. Anyway I knew that this man meant business and I would not talk or whisper to anyone. One day this cute brown nosing girl got caught talking and sure enough she got the strap. Then this very quiet Dutch girl got caught. We all felt sorry for her as she was only talking to answer what another girl had asked her. But true to his word he gave her the strap. The next day there was a great bang on the door and when Moose opened it a huge Dutch woman whacked him with an overhand right and down he went. The poor girl was so embarrassed and the big lady said if you ever touch my daughter again I will kill you, you son of a bitch. I really felt sorry for Moose because everyone had got fair warning.

Another big time strapper was Mr. Hawkins the metal teacher. One day Reg Irving and I got caught cheating on a metal work exam. He told Reg to roll up his sleeves and he hit him so hard across his wrists his veins swelled up out of his arms. He told me to pull up my sleeves and I told him simply "I don't do the strap sir". He sent me to the principal, Mr. Martin who understood that strapping was not part of my belief. I told you he was cool. He told me to cool it or I would have to move my desk into his office but told me not to quit school. You're a good man Harry.

When I first got to the school a councilor asked me if I wanted to go into a university program or a general program. I had no idea what he was talking about as I had never heard that terminology before. I guess he figured I was a moron so he put me in the general program. It was full of older bigger boys and attractive girls that had failed a few grades. They were my kind of people for sure. Div 7, how I loved it.

When I got to grade 10 it was even better as I joined up with a guy I had heard a lot about. His name was and still is Orville Boyd. He was a rock hard kid who was good at all sports including boxing. We knew of each other's reputation so when we first met it was a sort of strained congeniality. A few days later I talked to him and told him that if we rumble there will be a loser and that we should join forces as there were a lot of bullies from north Nanaimo that we would have to contend with. He agreed and we became and still are close friends. Within a week, a bad ass, who had just got out of jail, tried to jump me in class. Orville saw him sneaking up behind me and cold cocked him. Another day these airheads were throwing spitballs at each other and the guy in front of me ducked and it landed on my desk. He was another guy who had come straight from jail, he looked and he was tough. He looked at me and said "give me that spitball" as I was holding it. I just reached down and grabbed the bottom of his desk and flipped him over ass backward, then proceeded to boot the piss out of him while he was on the floor. We got hauled down to the vice principal who was an ex air force type. He told the other guy to try to do better and then told me that if I ever took my animal instincts out on any students again he would throw me out. I knew then that I would not get a fair hearing in the future.

He really had it for me because I hung around with Wino, who one day came to school with his head shaved, wearing jack boots and had swastika bands on his biceps. After the fight I went to the can to comb my hair and the other guy came in behind me and said that I did not give him a fair chance and he thought he could take me in a fair fight. I asked him if he wanted me to take his eye out with the rat tail comb I was using. I was just bluffing.

I had a lot of laughs that year with my buddies Vern, Bubbles, Orvie and Vic. But one day in mid May I was sitting at my desk and the study room teacher said to me as I was sleeping head down on my desk "Gogo, why do you bother coming to school?" I thought it was a fair question so I told him "being here is like being on a train, I just keep rolling along until I see a good spot to get off." It was a sunny day so I just got up and left and never came back. I was not pissed off at all but just realized it was time to move on. My mother was not happy.

BARE BALLS IN THE RIVER

A bunch of us boys about 14 years old would go up to a spot on the Nanaimo River between Christmas and New Year's. We would make a large bonfire and dare each other to jump into the cold water. There was always snow on the ground. Danny Ryn always won the contest as he could stay in the ice cold water far longer than any of us other boys. I can still hear his great laughter and picture his blue balls. Danny went on to become a successful realtor and had a kind and generous heart. Now departed, you were quite a guy big Dan.

Miss Vicki Ryn – Dan's beautiful sister

Ed Gogo and Mike Gogo in Carmanah Valley

DEANNA MCINTYRE

When I was about 14 I had a buddy that had a paper route. One of his deliveries was to a house on Shepard Street in Harewood. There was a girl living there name Deanna who was very petite. She was Scottish Italian cross and was very attractive with a bubbly personality. I actually used to help my pal with the newspapers just to see her. She was far more mature than I so it never went anywhere. She went on to become a successful business woman and now resides in Calgary. We get together about every 6 months and are often joined by a few of the other ladies from school. They are my Gogo girls.

The Right Honorable Bertha M. Metro

MY AUNTIE BERTHA

My mother was born in Stoke on Trent in jolly old England. Her father was a soldier serving in India with the Royal Horse Artillery. He immigrated to Canada with his wife and 4 children; a son, Roland and his 3 younger sisters Bertha, Phyllis "my mother" and Laura. He was killed in a mining accident in south Wellington near Nanaimo on February 9, 1915, along with 20 other coal miners. His widow Lucy was offered $1500 or tickets back to England. But as WW1 was on, ocean travel was dangerous so she built a modest house and struggled to support her 4 children. The house was just a shell and her son Roland had to go to work, at age 14 in the same coal mine that had just claimed his father. The eldest daughter, Bertha started working in the famous Empress Hotel in Victoria when she was a young girl. She moved to San Francisco in 1935 and took a job as a hotel chamber maid at $2.35 a day, 6 days a week, with zero benefits. One year later she founded local 283. She was 5'2" and 95 lbs. but when she spoke people listened.

In 1937, Local 283 struck San Francisco's hotels for 89 days, at the time the longest hotel strike in US history, and brought 4500 people into the union. She was always on the front lines. As the years went by she served on the Grand Jury and on the Fair Employment Practices Board. At a meeting with the millionaire owners of the hotels she told them "the maids in your hotels are the most important people in the house" if the room isn't right, the guests will never eat in their restaurants or drink in their bars. Many owners agreed with her and had great respect for her power and her integrity. Even in death she was giving as she donated her eyes.

When I was 21 I took my wife Judy to San Francisco to visit her and we went to a lunch the mayor hosted for her. We had lobster thermidor, a dish I had never heard of and the mayor was more than attentive as she represented a huge voting block and was a 100% democrat. She would come to Nanaimo to visit my mother every second summer and they would go to the Bengal Room at the Empress Hotel for their tea with all the English accompaniments. Now that is something to work in a hotel as a chamber maid and come back many years later as a US National Union Head. She told me when I was about 13, "Mickey, there are 2 kinds of people in the world, those who have assets and those who wish they had." Wishing was not her thing but doing sure as hell was. Of course I am greatly proud of her and the incredible amount of kindness she did for thousands of working people, no detail too small no person was unimportant to her. I have a big picture of her in my office and I look upon it fondly.

THE POLICE CORPORAL AND THE MISSING CATS

My mother hated cats to begin with but it all hit the fan when one day her brother Rolly brought over a beautiful steelhead salmon to be baked for dinner. My mother put it in the alcove which was a strange room in the back of the house where the weird combination of fine china and guns were stored. It was an unheated cold room so the salmon was placed on a newspaper to keep cold until it was time to put it in the oven. A cat clawed its way through the screen door and made a mess of the fish. My mom went ballistic and told me she would like to see, as she would say, the end of cats in this area. The next morning I got a peep site 22 and knocked off a shit load of marauding cats and buried them in the compost pile. A few days later an RCMP by the name of Corporal James knocked on our door and said a certain neighbor had complained about her missing cats and that I was the prime suspect. My mother told him that the last few days I had come straight home and spent the afternoons practicing piano. She also told him that he was the best singer that our parish had ever heard. To that he said "your son could not be responsible" and departed with a smile on his face that sported a fine waxed mustache. Mark one off for the "Dogans".

THE LACROSSE-PLAYING PEACH STEALERS

We had some good neighbours across the street that had two dandy big peach trees on the south side of the house, gleaning the sun rays. When the peaches were ripe we would throw our lacrosse ball into their yard near the peach trees and pretend that we were entering their yard to retrieve the ball, but when we got near the trees I would pick off a couple of peaches and throw them across the road to Monzi and then walk out the gate with the ball.

FENCE PICKETS
AND BLACK BAKED POTATOES

In the fall we would go a ways from our neighborhood and rip a few dry pickets off someone's fence and bring them back to our boulevard to make a fire. When the fire died down we would throw in a bunch of my dad's potatoes and someone would get a salt shaker. A half hour later the potatoes would be baked black and ready to eat. I can still smell and taste them.

TOMMY
AND LENNY

My father had 2 mechanics that worked on his logging equipment. Tommy was a diminutive man who had experience in the Arctic. I always remember the stories about how cold it was and that they had to keep everything running 24 hours a day or the equipment would freeze and not be able to start again. There was a lot of pressure on the men to make sure that all went well or huge problems could occur. Tommy was generous and helped me get my old Model A going (he did 99% of it). He loved sawing up enormous fir logs with an old McCullough chain saw. He would stand on a huge round of timber and split it with a steel wedge and axe. He looked like a little woodpecker chopping on the big rounds. Lenny was a complete piss tank and I say that with love as he was a red faced man who could hardly stand up he was so corned. But he could fix anything and all he wanted was a few bucks for more booze. It was a shame as he could repair any car mechanical or bodywork. He loved my dad and used to say to him "Martha ya bugger, you're a good man". God rest their kind souls.

MR. DUNCAN'S OUTHOUSE

As I previously stated my father owned the whole block and we had our house on one end, a huge garden in the middle and on the other end of the block he rented out a small house to an old prairie farmer named Mr. Duncan. Mr. Duncan had an outhouse about 60 feet behind his house where, on New Year's Eve, with my brothers Ed and Danny, we shot holes through it. Sheer madness it was and many times I have thought what if the old boy had been in there unbeknownst to us. It makes me cringe when I think about that.

DON'T SHOOT THE PHEASANT

I was always trying to bag a nice cock pheasant as some beauties used to come into our garden. I told my dad about my plan but he told me that they are such beautiful birds he did not want me to shoot them. Of course I did not listen and one day I had one lined up in the sights of a 22 rifle. As I was pulling the trigger my dad came out or nowhere and tapped me on the shoulder and said "don't shoot the pheasants'. Man was he ever patient with me.

I used to like the smell of gasoline and I used to sniff the empty gas barrels. I now understand how toxic it is but in those days we did not know any better, in fact people washed car parts in gasoline with their bare hands.

DON'T PISS THE BED

One night I was dreaming I was urinating but the reality was obvious when I woke up in a wet bed. I was of course embarrassed as hell and tried to hide it from my mother by making the bed. She really raised hell with me when she found out. I sure remember that.

FISHING AND BEE STINGS

I used to love going fishing by myself on the Chase River and one of my favorite spots was beside a big cedar tree whose roots hung over the riverbank. While fishing there one summer day, I started to jump up and down on the roots as they were like a spring. That turned out to be a bad idea as unbeknownst to me there was a nest of yellow jackets under those roots. The next thing I know there was a cloud of bees all over me and they stung the hell out of me. I remember coming home and my mother putting this product called Blueing all over me. I hate wasps (and right wing Catholics as well).

HALF CRUCIFIED
IN THE BARN

There was an old hay barn about 2 blocks from where I lived on 303 Fifth St. A group of us young boys would go there and leap off the top of the rafters and land in the soft hay. We loved it. One day, as the farmer fed out the hay to his cattle, the pile of hay of course got smaller until finally there were only a few feet of hay left on the barn floor. I took a dive off the rafters and when I landed my hand went down through the hay onto the floor where there was a nail sticking up through the floor. The nail went right through the palm of my hand. I went home and I remember my dad washing it out with soap and water then pouring iodine on it. Now that hurts! The only other time that I ever jumped that high is the one time that I ever caught my member in my zipper. As the old story goes "no man has ever stood as tall as the man who got his unit caught in his zipper". Truth is, getting it out that is the real test of courage.

I LOVE CHRISTMAS

Like most other children, Christmas was the highlight of the year for me. With such a large family we had presents piled up high around the tree. My oldest brother Ken would pick up a present, announce the person's name and we would wait for the person to open it. It took hours but I loved it. Christmas dinner, great deserts and Alastair Simms as Scrooge in "A Christmas Carol" on TV; happy, happy, happy.

EARL THE GYPSY

One of the kids I used to play with was Earl a gypsy boy. We were not allowed to go to his house or into his yard. This embarrassed him and he came out to play whenever his parents, who I cannot remember ever seeing, let him out of the house. They moved here from Vancouver and one day many years later I was reading The Vancouver Sun and noticed an article that stated "Man Charged With Prostitution". I read the article and sure enough it was about Earl. Apparently he was picked up in Vancouver on a prostitution charge as he was wearing women's clothes but when they took him to jail they found he had the complete package. If my memory serves me correctly his lawyer had him plead not guilty as the dictionary definition of prostitution is "a sexual favor from a woman for a man in exchange of money". In any event the judge was not buying into that argument so Earl hit the bucket.

SHOOTING THE OWL

One day a bunch of us kids were playing outside when we spotted a big snow owl chasing a wounded seagull. The owl could not catch him so he landed on top of a neighbors clothesline pole. We all ran in and told my dad and he took his old single barrel 12 gauge shotgun and we all went behind him like he was the pied piper. The owl was perched up on top of the Colson's clothes line pole. Dad smoked him and we took it to the taxidermist. When he was ready we put him on the mantel piece where he perched for a good many years. If someone shot an owl like that today it would be on the national news and at least 3 or 4 government agencies would be involved and of course we children would need a trauma councilor. What a crock!

THE MEXICAN CREDIT CARD

Our gang, Dan, Gerald, Vern, Ron, Pat and I used to
go out at night and siphon gas out of people's
vehicles. We used a 5 gallon can and an 8' piece of
garden hose. We called it our Mexican credit card.
One night a few of the boys were doing their thing as
we all had a quota to get 10 gallons each by the
weekend. We would use this for our car or sell it for
cash. One night my brother Dan and I were sitting in
a car a block away from 2 of our buddies who were
siphoning gas. We had already filled our quota and
were waiting for the 2 other lads to get theirs.
Someone in the area dropped a dime and the police
started cruising the area. They came up behind our
car, arrested us and threw us in jail for the night. I
remember my brother Dan singing the old Kingston
Trio song "Tijuana Jail" half the night. The next day
we were in front of old "Potsy" the stern old local
Magistrate who had in my opinion zero mercy for
anyone. He wanted to put us in reform school for 2
years but our asses were saved by the local prosecutor
Mr. Healy who was a thoroughly decent old cop who
doubled as a prosecutor. Mr. Healy insisted that we
were good boys from a good family and that
incarceration was not necessary. The fact that we

were never caught doing anything illegal was not an issue as the Kangaroo Court ruled the land. In any event, thanks again to Mr. Healy, we were released into the custody of my brother Ken who drove us back up to the farm. As we approached the farmhouse he said he had it in mind to give us a good thrashing. We laughed at him and said that for his sake that would not be a good idea. We got 18 months of probation and I remember this probation officer coming to the farm one day unannounced to check on us. That particular day Dan and I had put on these old black trench coats and were hiding in a drainage ditch to shoot some pigeons that were raiding our newly planted oat fields. When he arrived we walked out to where he was with our hillbilly hats, double barrel shotguns wearing black trench coats. He was a Baptist Minister and part time probation officer. He took one look at us and excused himself and we never heard from him again.

STEALING BLACKBERRIES AT MR. MIROSLAVES

I used to pick a hell of a lot of blackberries for my mother. I prided myself on never having under or overripe berries and no dandelion fluff or stems. Surprisingly I never ate any either. I just picked until my big milk bucket was full and rounded on top. My mother made wonderful pies, jams and jellies. I went all over the neighborhood hanging off chicken coops and peoples garage roofs to get the biggest, ripest ones. Every so often I would sneak down the alley to Mr. Miroslaves back yard where he trained blackberries to grow on vines. Man they were loaded. I used to pop the nails on the bottom of 1 single picket, swing the board sideways and get my skinny little body through. Ten furious minutes of picking and I was gone until next time.

RAFTING ON THE CREEK

I built a small raft down on the bank of the Chase River where I would go rafting in the summer, such fun it was. I remember one day a bunch of us boys were there and we would throw a stick in the water upstream and then throw rocks at it as it sailed down the river. I must have stepped in front of another boy as I was hit on the crown of my head by a rock. It bled a lot and I remember going to a house near the creek and knocking on their door with very bloody hands. To this day, I blame that mishap for my insanity

CAROL'S UNDERPANTS ON THE CLOTHESLINE

When I was about 10 years old we heard the older boys talking about pretty girls and their underpants or some such thing. We thought this girl named Carol who lived down the street was very pretty, but how were we going to see her underpants? I thought that if we lifted her dress we would get in trouble so I came up with the idea that if we waited for her mother to put out the wash on the clothesline they would surely be there. So one morning, out came the laundry and we stood in the alleyway staring at the gonchies, but we could not figure out what the attraction was. Her mother came out and asked us what we were doing so we ran away.

MY SISTER LAURA AND THE GIBSON GIRLS

When I was about 12 my sister Laura used to have the Gibson sisters stay over on Friday night, as by that time some of my older brothers and sisters had gotten married and moved out so there was room for sleepovers. Carol was the oldest, then Louise, and Marybell. They were very pretty girls and on Saturday they would use me as their model and practice putting makeup on me. I used to love the attention and all their giggles. Where were they 5 years later when I would have liked the attention even more?

Mickey – the young logger at 17

Left: Rick (Bowhack) Bowick
Middle: Mickey
Right: Gerald Patrick (Wino)
Winemaster
Note: His affectionate grasp
on the gallon of Berrycup wine

THE BEST FRIEND EVER – "MAD DOG"

His real name was Gerald Patrick Winemaster but I called him "Wino" and he was known to all others as "Mad Dog" Nazi Winemaster. In life we all meet people we call friends but there is always one who is "the guy", and that was "Wino". I met him in grade

10 and we became instant friends. He had a command of the English language that was second to none. Pat's father was a successful Texaco Oil Executive who I admired as he had put himself through university and always drove a beautiful convertible that he traded in every 2 years. Unfortunately Pat never got along with Gerry senior as no doubt his dad wanted Wino to conform and get into business. That was not ever going to happen as Wino was all about well, wine. He was a great artist who could draw a portrait of anyone in minutes. He was a loner as a kid so he sat and read the dictionary all the time. He told me he did this to put down his father. It was the one thing that he could use to demonstrate his superiority in at least one thing. Pat was a big guy and could be intimidating but never fought with anyone as he was somewhat of a pacifistic. He could insult someone using a string of words that most of us had never heard. In time we developed a language that no one else could understand, a type of Pig Latin if you will. We wore the same size of clothes and he would say "whoever gets up first gets the best clothes".

We batched together and he would clean up and I would cook. We once lived in a 51 Hardtop Ford for 3 months, me in the front and him in the back. He was always in great humor. I have seen him get out of the car early on a spring day, take a bar of soap and walk into a cold creek and have a bath. He said that he had read that the smell of a man's perspiration was attractive to females but we were certainly pushing the limit so into the cold water he went, and not for a minute but until he felt clean.

It was a laugh a minute and nothing was too outrageous for us to do. Some of the things we did will remain unpublished as who knows the legal time limits on the dastardly deeds we preformed. I have never experienced any exhilaration like heading to parts unknown in a 51 Mercury hard top with a full tank of gas, a case of Prem, a case of canned spaghetti and two gallons of homemade wine in an old stone jug - total freedom. We really had no clue where we were going other than it was always north in the springtime. A great duo, we were dumb and dumber on steroids. There are so many stories but even after close to 50 years I still do not believe the world is ready to read them.

One story I can tell is when we were going through Smithers and stopped at a garage store to buy some Wagon Wheels. Do you remember them? They were these huge round biscuit-type of chocolate bars; at that time they were 5 cents. We went into the store and meet an American kid, about 17, who had gone A-wall from the US Army. He said he could not tolerate discipline. We said he could join us as we had the same beliefs and he was hungry and friendless. Just as we were ready to leave the store and get back in the car we saw a group of about 7 or 8 local yokels who had it in their mind to kick the shit out of us because they thought they could. We discussed our plight for a minute and decided on a strategy. We walked calmly toward the car and when they made their move Pat pulled out his switch blade knife and made them freeze. The yank Billy, who was an Oki, and I kicked two of them in the balls and started wailing on two more. Wino kept the rest away with his knife. When we hammered the second two the rest jammed out and we were free to go. Billy was lightening quick and leather tough and figured that he has been pushed enough. There was a lot of blood in the gravel around the gas pumps, some of it ours but most of it theirs, so he was a welcome addition to our mayhem on wheels. I can remember the colour of the Skeena River as we drove along the highway. It looked like a billion gallons of Aqua Velva running through the valleys as it was the same colour, cold and pure from the mountains. I kept in touch with Billy for a few years but Wino pulled off a huge scam and went to Columbia where I understood he was killed in a gun fight. I loved those guys and believe because we had so much fun we should come back as ourselves and carry on with our madness. What great buddies I had.

MY FIRST DEER

One evening when I was 13 my 14 year old brother Dan and I were staying at Grandpa's cabin on the farm. We had a little 22 rifle and were sitting in two old wooden chairs under a big fir tree waiting in the late summer evening for a deer to come into the field. Sure enough along comes a spike buck. I took aim, fired and down went the deer. We were delighted and soon did a crude job of cleaning it. We used to open the chest cavity with a meat saw and hang it in a tree when you could then cut certain parts loose and all the offal just drops right down the neck, it really works slick. No blood and no mess. In subsequent years we shot dozens and dozens as they would eat and destroy any and all products we tried to grow. Fortunately my favorite meal is venison sausage and I never get tired of it. It contains 75% venison and 25% pork with a lot of garlic, Yum! Dip it in some HP sauce and you're in heaven.

GRANDPA'S CABIN

Dan and I would stay in Grandpa's cabin. It was small only about 12' x 20' but it had everything we needed. I can still smell the firewood, bacon grease, coffee and sweaty clothes. A carbide or coal oil lamp was our light at night. No running water so we had to walk down to an old well about ½ a mile away and get a bucketful of water to put on top of the old woodstove to heat up for dishwater and a big old kettle full for making tea. We would sleep in sleeping bags that one could buy from Simpson Sears for $13 dollars. In the winter it was not uncommon to see ice on top of the water in the bucket in the morning as when the fire burnt out it got cold. It was a lot colder back then. I remember plugging up the pipe coming out of the potato field with a piece of plywood and overnight the 5 acre potato field would flood and then freeze in a few days so we could skate on it and play hockey and the ice stayed hard for at least 6 weeks. We would build a big crackling bonfire beside the field and cook things over the fire. We always used a long fork stick to toast them. We'd have a few beers as well if we could get some. Sometimes my friend Orville, the boxer, would bring some girls up and we would skate for hours and then warm up by the fire. What a great way for young people to grow up.

My Dad – John Harold Gogo with a cougar

..................with his pet steer Ruffus

BETTER GET YOUR
EYES CHECKED POPCORN

Sometimes I would call my dad Popcorn as some kids called their father Pop. He was 48 when I was born so he was very mellow. One night I went pit lamping with him in our orchard to get a deer or two. He actually had a license to pit lamp and I have won many a bet by wagering this fact and I have a plasticized copy of it. Pit lamping is simply hunting at night with a flashlight. It mesmerizes the deer when the light is on them. The proper way is the shooter kneels down and his partner holds the light over his shoulder from behind. You shine your light on the deer and with the light from behind the shooter can clearly see the sights on his gun and the deer. It is the job of the light holder to see what transpires after the gun fires as the flash from the gun temporarily blinds the shooter. But the person holding the light can see the reaction of the deer. After many years the light holder gets very adept at which way the deer runs if it runs at all. One night there were several pairs of eyes in the branches of this apple tree that was loaded with transparent species of apples. I told dad that those eyes were not from a deer but he just said hold the light steady so I did. He let fly with both barrels of his fox 12 gauge shotgun. There was blood, raccoon feces, hair and guts all over the apples and tree. I realized then that Popcorn was in another world and I still laugh about it. It seems that I could not make the point with him that deer don't sit in trees.

BYE-BYE "IKE" THE BULLDOG

Probably the greatest shock of my childhood was the day I shot the neighbor's bulldog Ike. I hated that dog because it stank and was always sleeping in front of the neighbors' front door. That was a problem for me because I played with the boy next door and when I came to his front door it would wake up the cranky old piece of crap. One day he grabbed my calf and punctured my leg. Anyhow our house had about 20 guns, elk guns, deer guns, geese guns, pheasant guns, everything but an elephant gun. I used to play with them and there is one that caught my fancy. It was my brother Ron's gun called an Over & Under. It was a gun with 2 barrels one on top of the other. The top barrel was a 22 caliber and the bottom was a 410 gauge, a smaller shotgun size. The idea being you could use the 22 for deer and the shotgun for pheasants or grouse. Anyway I put a shotgun shell in the bottom of the gun, why I will never know, and a BB cap, which is a 22 shell with a fine shot like a shotgun but not one solid piece of lead. I figured that one day Ike would be strutting down the alleyway and I could give him a good dusting with the fine shot of a BB cap. I kept the gun under my bed to be ready if the opportunity presented itself. One morning I saw him coming down the alley about 50 feet from my bedroom window. I grabbed my gun and stuck it out my bedroom window and when Ike trotted by I blasted him in the ribcage. Problem was that the bottom barrel was activated so the shotgun shell fired and I killed old Ike. Can you imagine the look on my face as Ike's ribcage disintegrated in front of my eyes? Believe it or not I did not get in shit from my parents. The neighbor came to our home and was livid, but my dad said "we did not shoot your dog but it was time somebody did as it terrorized all the kids in the neighborhood" and he told him to bugger off! I still can't believe I got away with it.

THE GOLD PANNER

When I was about 13 there was a man who used to sluice for gold in a spot that we used to swim in on the Nanaimo River. He used to get the gold that got stuck behind the big rocks that were in the river bed. He told me the back eddies would whirl the gold in behind these big rocks and that he got about 1oz a day. In those days gold was pegged at around $27 per once and he said that he could make $32 a day as a sawyer in the Chemainus Sawmill, so he only did the gold work in the summer weekends when the water was low.

MEL SAVES MY ASS

The last year that I attended high school, come to think of it, it was also the first year, which was grade 10. I was walking down the hallway to my homeroom and someone stepped on my heel from behind. I paid no attention as I figured it was just some clumsy bugger, but then I received another very hard blow to my heel. I thought I don't care who it is doing this and it hurt like hell so I turned around and punched the person behind me as fast and as hard as I could. I hit the person in the throat and down he went. To my surprise it was a teacher. He was an arrogant cocky little bastard who thought I was too slow and in his way. He was really pissed off and started yelling that I was going to be expelled and he was going to phone the police and have me arrested. Little did I know that my homeroom teacher was standing in the hallway just outside of his classroom and saw everything that had happened. He told the other teacher that he had witnessed everything and he did not advise him to pursue the matter. Then he said "Michael, go sit in your seat." Gotta love Mel.

A BOY WHO LOVED FISHING

When I was a little boy about 12 my dad was logging in the Boulder Creek area and during the summer holidays I would sometimes go with him and climb down the very steep banks of the creek to go fishing. There were some big log jams in the creek and the water would store up in the deeper hole in front of the logs. I used no worms or lure only a very tiny hook that I would bate with salmon berries or huckleberries as they look just like salmon roe. I would put a little split shot "lead weight" about 8" from the hook and then slowly let it down into the cold shaded deep holes. What excitement it was for me to see a big plump trout sneak out from below the log jam and take the bait. I would let it go with the bait and swallow the tiny barbed hook and then a slight pull on the line and bango!!! I had him and I would flip him out onto the creek bank. Again, what a thrill to see a big trout stealthfully sneak out of hiding and slowly take the bait, huge anticipation on my part. A young boy peering down into the log jam with a fishing rod in his hand would have been a good Norman Rockwell painting. When I landed the trout I would put it on a gill stick and for the 99% of you that don't know what that is I will explain. You break a small branch off of an alder tree about 2 feet long and you take all the side limbs off it except the one at the bottom. You thread the stick through the gills of the fish and then put the stick with the fish attached back into the cool stream and anchor it down with a rock. This keeps them fresh and cool.

HOW I GOT TO TOWN

When we moved out to the farm I was about 14 so of course I wanted to get to town some evenings during the week, but was not allowed and I had no way of getting there other than walking the 7 miles down a very dark gravel road with deep potholes full of water. I walked it a few times on a Friday night but gave up on that as my shoes would get filled up with water from the deep potholes in the road. It was black as coal in the forested area so you could not see the holes. I figured a way to get to town on the odd night that my brother Ed and my dad went to the Terminal Hotel for a beer. I would hide in the trunk of the car and when they got to the parking lot I would push the backseat forward and unlock the back door and get out. I knew that they would leave to go back to the farm about 11p.m. so I made sure that I was back in the trunk by 10:30.

OUTRUN THE COPS

One day I was heading down the mountain with a nice two point buck slung over the hood of my pickup, as was the custom of the day to give to a family in Harewood. As I passed the SPCA I was met by a car full of RCMP officers who were going to the rifle range to practice. I could see them turning around in my rear view mirror so I gunned it down Nanaimo Lakes Road in my 52 Ford ½ ton that I had bought for $75. I made a hard, fast right on Wakesiah Ave and then left down 6th street. I could see to both sides of me so I gunned it through the stop sign and headed down to Budda's place. I drove down a side road over a hill and down into a big pile of blackberry bushes. It was quite a ride. I left the truck there for a month as I knew the cops would be pissed off by being outrun by a 52 Flathead Ford. I had no hunting license, no deer tags and I'm sure there were a dozen things wrong with my truck, so getting stopped was not an option.

SONNY

One of the nicest guys I had ever met was Dick Rassmuson. We all called him Sonny. He was a great guy, he was funny and very objective about

everything. When there would be a dispute amongst us, he would break out the boxing gloves and the two guys disputing
would go at it. Afterward he would make the two combatants shake hands. He was wise and mature beyond his years. Sadly Sonny drove by my place one day and committed suicide by jumping in Nanaimo River. He was about 45 and it broke my heart.

PISSING IN THE VAPOUR PAN

One day when I was a kid about 11 years old, my older brothers told me to go and put some wood on the furnace. My parents had gone shopping that Saturday and because I was quite spoiled I had never done this job before. They kicked my ass down to the basement to do the job so I pissed in the vapor pan to stink them out of the house. I took a beating for that stunt.

PATIENT CATHY
AND LUCIEN THE ASSHOLE

When my brother Ron got
married he and his wife
Cathy moved into a suite
in our basement. She
came from a great family
and was so patient with
me when I was a kid.
When we watched TV
together I must have
asked her a thousand

questions. Cathy what does this mean and what does
that mean? She never got pissed off with me and she
helped me probably more than most teachers. On the
other hand my sister Marilyn married a French
Canadian name Lucien. He tried to be sort of an
authoritarian big brother to my brother Dan and me.
It was not appreciated as we had all the big brothers
we needed. One day at the family dinner table he
tried to make me eat beef or venison meat but at the
time I would only eat hotdogs. He sat next to me
after supper and would not let me leave the table until
I ate the meat. After about an hour he said he would
eat half if I would eat the other half so I agreed but
when he ate his half I once again refused to eat my
half. We sat there for another hour until he had to go
to the can. When he left I quickly dumped it over the
back porch railing. When he came back the plate was
empty so he looked in the garbage under the sink but
could find nothing. I could not stand the man. My
sister always came over for Sunday dinner and he
would bore my poor mother with his bullshit stories
while smoking one cigarette after the other.

DAVY AND MONZI

I used to love boxing and I got some good lessons from my buddies Davy Taylor and Kenny Maughans. Davy was fast as lightning and Ken was a great counter puncher who most always put me on the canvas. I should have sold advertising on the bottom of my shoes. There was a kid that lived a few blocks away named Dan Ryn. He was big and tough and one day we met at the neighborhood playground. He walked up to me and slapped me hard in the face. I had never even met him before, so the fight was on. I got him down and pounded him good but whenever I

let him up he started swinging again. I finally got so tired I had to go get my friend Sonny Rasmusson to sit on Dan until I could get my breath back. A few years later Dan moved close to my house and we became the best of friends. His sister Vicky is a most pleasant lady and a real sweetie.

WHERE IS JOE CATULOW

Bubbles and I would pull off some random shenanigans and when it was done we would tell people that it was Joe Catulow, a guy just over from Vancouver. The police were always questioning people about his whereabouts. This went on for a year or two and then we cooled it. We called it Catulowism.

John and Phyllis (mom and dad)
*** – strutting their stuff in Seattle***
*** – mid 3o's***

Back 1st person – Cousin George Saam
Back middle – Cousin Eddie Saam
Back right – John Gogo (Dad)
Front – Uncle George Metro

LIFE ON THE FARM

My mother and father moved from our home on 5th Street in Harewood when I was about 14. We moved to my Grandfathers farm about 12 miles from Nanaimo. It was great, the school bus dropped me off in Extension about 4 miles from the farm and my brother Dan who is 14 months older than me would ride down with an extra horse and we would race home. There were only 3 boys left at home when mom and dad moved back to the farm. One day I looked at the supper table and saw our ham, potatoes, carrots and peas, bread, butter and blackberry pie and commented that everything on the table other than the salt and pepper was either grown by my father or cooked by my mother. Us boys of course contributed greatly by eating it all. My mother and father had 8 children and 37 grandchildren. How's that for Roman roulette?

I CAN'T MAKE SOUP OUT OF TRACKS

One day when I was about 15 my dad handed me a gun and told me to go out and shoot some deer because they were eating all of his garden plants. I have even seen them going right down a row of potatoes and pushing them out with their front feet. I walked around the farm for a couple of hours and did not see any deer as basically they are a night feeding animal. I told my dad that I did not see any deer but that I had seen a lot of tracks. He laughed at me and asked me how can he make soup out of tracks?

My feelings were hurt so I asked my brother Ron who was a great hunter about deer hunting. Over the next year I shot 38 deer. I used to bone them out. My dad used to dress blue and willow grouse and make a coating and fry them up. They were delicious and we called it blue chicken. My parents were great people and I was more than lucky to have been born to them.

THEFT AT THE #14 HOUSE

We only lived about 2 blocks from the old Nanaimo Chinatown. It was a huge place that covered about 40 acres. It was just like a town you see in the cowboy movies. Two story buildings, hitching posts in front of the stores with board sidewalks in front. It was a wonderful place to live close to as you could buy firecrackers 7 days a week in #14 House which was way down the left side of the main street. There was a very old Chinese man that would always bring out a box of various firecrackers and we would buy maybe 10 cents worth. One day Greg Fox and I decided to steal the box and get away quickly on our bikes. We planned it for a long time and one day we went there as usual and when he brought out the box we grabbed it off the counter and Greg put it in the carrier of his bike. We peddled away as fast as possible with the poor man yelling at us as we scurried down the street. All hell broke out and there were men trying to stop us as we whisked by them. Greg's bike hit a pothole and the box of firecrackers went straight up in the air and landed behind him on the street. I never showed my face around there until about a year later when I went to the Puss in Boots Café. There was an electric game there with a gun and you could shoot at rabbits in the background. It was 10 cents a game and that is all I had but the owner would let me play a couple more games for free as he was very kind. I think it was Chuck Wong but I can't remember. Of course Chuck, Gunner and Henry Wong went on to build the Diners Rendezvous Café in downtown Nanaimo after the big Chinatown fire circa app 1961. The Wong brothers were the world's most hospitable people. After 45 years they closed due to old age.

It was "the place" to go when I was a teenager. It was funny to see all the booths where you could see big grease spots against the wall of each booth as all the boys had their hair loaded with Brylcream and their greasy heads would leave a sizable stain on the wallpaper.

One day when I was a teenager, a guy from Vancouver who had recently joined our gang came in very drunk and was abusive to the youngest brother, Henry. I felt I had to intervene even though Henry could really duke it out if necessary. I felt it was my responsibility as he was new to our gang. I told Rick to cool it as he was already on probation but he would not listen and he took a swing at me. I picked him up and slammed him down on someone's table and knocked the wind out of him then took him home before someone phoned the police. That was on a Saturday night and on Monday I was in Magistrates Court on a minor traffic charge. The judge Eric Winch asked me if I had been behaving these days and I assured him I was. He said well it did not look like it last Saturday night at The Rendezvous when you threw that guy on top of my table. What could I say?

There are a thousand stories about The Rendezvous. They were all the most congenial people that I ever met. When Henry was dying I went to the hospital a couple of times to visit. He was always unconscious but would phone the next day and say how sorry he was to have missed me and thank me for coming to see him. The oldest brother Chuck used to take an hour to make me this huge bowl of curried chicken and always had a little gift for my lady friend. He used to say to people "Mike Gogo, few want to fight him". My last memory of the place I was sitting with Chuck and Henry and telling them of my romantic quests in Cuba when an old man who was there looked at me and said "you've never been to Brazil have you, kid ?"

POP HAWKINS

As I got older and stronger I had new ways to make a dollar, I took my sister Laura's bike and could put a 100 lb. sack of potatoes in the V part and walk it down the street and sell the sack of potatoes to a neighbor for $3.00. My dad grew tons of them on the farm and I could take a sack now and then and have some legitimate spending money.

The man who taught me a lot was old Pop Hawkins. He was a wheeler dealer if there ever was one. He was a little short man who wore a big cowboy hat. He had a million stories and when I was about 13 he phoned me and asked me if I wanted to make some money. He told me to ride my bike over to his place right away. He asked me the dimensions, in feet, of an acre of land and I admitted I did not know so he told me I was ignorant. Then he asked me what kind of eating corn grew the best in this climate but of course I had not a clue. Once again he told me I was ignorant. I guess he could see that I was getting a little disparaged so he told me that I was not stupid but only ignorant and he was going to teach me how to always stand behind a round table. I was to learn that if you stand behind a round table no one could ever corner or catch you. So he said here is $2.00 now go to Percy Leasks hardware store just down the alley and buy me a big ball of string. I brought it back to him and he told me to go and cut 4 sturdy sticks about

2" thick and 2 feet long. He then instructed me to pound one of them into the ground about a foot deep. He had me measure off a piece of the string 212' long. He had me tie the string to the second wooden stake and so on until we had a perfect square. He then said "Do you know what this is?" I replied that I did not."its one acre" was his reply "so now you know". He then named 3 people that did rotovating with a farm tractor and I was to use his phone and contact them about pricing to rotovate this 1 acre lot plot. I was to tell each man that the land had to be rotovated a second time, one week after the first time, but it must be done on a sunny day on the second go around. He told me that the second rotovation would

kill most of the weeds but only if it was sunny.

Once the tractor operator gave me a price and went to get his tractor Pop got me to move the stakes out about 5 feet so we got a bonus on the rotovating. I still had no clue as to where I stood in all of this but when the rotovating was done the second time around the ground was like flour. He then gave me money to go to the feed store and buy 5 pounds of Golden Cross Bantman Seed Corn. After I did that he instructed me to use the same string to mask out the rows for planting. He showed me how deep and how far apart the corn seeds should be planted. He never did anything physical it was only verbal instructions. Soon the corn started to sprout so he had me hoe down the weeds but only on a sunny day. An acre is a lot for a kid to hoe so one day I asked him when we would make some money from this. He told me "when it's ready of course". When the corn got to be about a foot high Pop told me not to hoe it anymore as the corn would outgrow the weeds and we then wait for it to ripen. When the corn was at the height of ripeness Pop got me to put a big carrier basket on my bike and at 7:00 a.m. the next morning he showed me how to pick the cobs. I was to put 13 cobs in each bag then drive down the street and knock on every door. When the lady answered, who mostly always had her housecoat and slippers on as most women at that time did not work out of the house, I would open a cob right in front of her to show her that it was just perfect. If you know anything about corn you will know it is best before the last kernels ripen on the end of the cob. The corn was 60 cents a dozen and one cob on the house. If she would take 3 dozen "put two in the freezer" she got them for 50 cents a dozen. On my best day I sold 120 dozen and I got to keep 50% of the money. Pop said he paid for the rotovating and corn and I did the planting and hoeing so it was 50/50 on sales. Hey I was rich. The next year he phoned to see if I was ready to do it again but I said that my dad would give me an acre so I could do it on my own. He laughed and said "you're learning".

One day I was bugging Pop, Alf was his name, saying I wanted to learn how to buy and sell livestock. He said okay and gave me a dollar and said that I have to go around to the farms and buy 3 chickens with the dollar so I put a potato sack in my carrier and away I went. No one would sell me 3 chickens for a dollar as 50 cents each was as low as they would go. I then found an old goat rancher about 4 miles away, who after much negotiating agreed to sell me 3 for a dollar. I put them in my gunny sack and pedaled the long road to Pop's farm. I got Pop out of his house and took the sack over to a shed so my precious chickens would not escape, but when I opened the sack to release them he just stared at me and shook his head and yelled "Mickey, those are Bantams and you can buy them anywhere for 3 for a dollar". I was tired and very disappointed and just sat down on a bale of hay and cried for a long time. After I was finished blubbering Pop came back and said to me most sternly "Listen kid, you have just learned a cheap lesson and a lot of men have paid a lot more for their first lesson."

When I was older I would drive a little cattle truck to livestock auctions and he would buy all the runt pigs for next to nothing and then sell them as a litter of young wiener pigs as they were all the same size. Another trick was to buy a cow that was at the end of her lactating cycle for a small cost. Then not milk her for a few days so it looked like she was a freshened cow, then throw in a calf that was easily bought for a very few dollars and usually free from dairyman as they got rid of the bull calves the day they were born, as they only kept female calves. He would put the cow that by this time had a full milk bag, together with the calf and sold them as a cow and calf pair which brought top dollar.

Love ya Pop, for all you taught me.

NOT SAFE SEX

When I was about 15 there was a very busty and rambunctious girl who lived in a little, all but abandoned, former mining town called Extension. She was built like the proverbial outhouse and always had a smile. We used to meet at this old Italian dairy farmer's barn and we would horse around, all puns intended. One day, we were swinging on a rope together in the loft of the barn when the rope gave way from a rafter. We went crashing along the floor and slid to a stop only a few inches from going over the edge of the open top door and falling 30 feet down to a cement-floored corral. It scared me so much that I never went back, well okay, maybe a few times. The old farmer that owned the place was Dominick Armanasko who was about as kind as any man could be and gave me excellent council on a number of occasions.

5 CENTS A GAME

When I was about 14 I worked at night as a pinsetter in a bowling alley and we were paid 5 cents a game to set the 5 pins on the spikes. It was a stinky job as the boys used to piss where they worked because they could not stop when there were customers playing the game.

The owner was a miserable old bastard that would not let me store my bike in the big storage area so I was always worried about getting my bike stolen from the parking lot. In the late Spring, people did not come in as much so you could not get in 20 games most nights so you made less than $1.00. So I took the job of janitor that paid $1.00 a night. I had to wash the floors, clean and wash the ashtrays, clean the bathrooms and sweep the hallways and sort and store away the pop bottles and bag the trash.

I saved enough to buy a 22 rifle, a sleeping bag and saved $40.00 cash. One night an older bigger boy was trying to bully me into giving him my PEP chocolate bar so I waited until he was bent over setting pins when I nailed him across the head with a 5 pin. I broke his nose and I got fired but I didn't care as I had everything that I wanted.

THE CHOCOALTE MILK MAN

One day when my brother Dan and I were about 10 years old we were walking home from the convent school and heard all this clinking noise behind a building on Fitzwilliam Street. We discovered a man bottling chocolate milk. I guess he could see the look on our faces because he gave us each a pint to drink, it was cold and delicious. He told us that we could come by everyday as long as we did not bring more kids. I saw him many years later at a hockey game and walked up to him to thank him but he did not remember me.

Man, that cold chocolate milk was delicious. Just another random act of kindness.

OLD CURLY THE BARBER

There was an older barber named Curly McNeil who had a little barber shop in town. He was a half ass relative of our family. When my brother Dan and I were young boys we would go there for a haircut and he always refused payment. He was a very kind man who used to go to the hospital and cut the hair of poor people and veterans for free.

He used to take me fishing for Bass on Quesnel Lake when I was about 12 years old. One day I was pushing the raft we were fishing from with a long pole and the pole got stuck in the mud and I walked off the end of the raft into the lake. Old Curly laughed about that for years saying "Mickey takes a long walk on a short raft". He used to pretend that he was spitting in his hand and he would then rub it on our hair before he would do the final combing and trimming.

God bless his kind, caring and gentle soul.

DRUGS

I have never even tried any drugs. After all they call it "dope", don't they?

When I was a little boy, I noticed that old Chinese men always planted a huge amount of poppies in our flower gardens. One day I asked my Dad if he pays them to work in our yard. He said that they were growing opium poppies and in the late summer they harvested the plants to use for the production of opium. He said that thousands of young Chinese men came to Canada and worked at hard and dangerous jobs and were without the comforts of a happy married life as they sent most of their money home to China so their families could get a piece of land to grow food to feed their families.

Sadly, the Communist Government took their land and killed millions of farm owners. All the lifetime toils of the local men were in vain. He, of course, saw it as it was a huge crime to the Chinese farmers.

Dad told me that now the local old Chinese men were old and full of rheumatism from their age and exposure to the cold working conditions in mining and forestry. He reasoned that why should these poor men have to buy expensive drugs from local drugstores to alleviate their pain when they could grow their own.
I am sure that the pain in their hearts was every bit as severe as the pain in their joints. A lifetime of toil for naught.

THE HORNEY GIRL AND MY BELT

When I was about 15, I met this wild child named Josephine. She was incredibly exciting to be with as she was always nibbling on my ear, etc.
She was a year or two older than me so that put me into the major leagues in my mind. All was going great until one night at our evening dinner table. My father never did have the "Birds and Bees" talk with me. I guess he thought I should have got my sex education listening to the older boys in the pool hall. He exclaimed for all the family to hear , " I got a call

from Mr. (shall remain nameless) today and he told me that you are making a nuisance of yourself at his house". I said nothing, but thought that if he knew the action to be had there he may not have insisted on my celibacy at that address. Apparently, her two younger sisters had witnessed me climbing in Jose's window one night and thank goodness did not rat her out until the next day.

So here is the big story. One day in her bedroom she told me that she wanted to have something of mine to be with her at all   times and she asked me if she could have my belt for that purpose. My ego soared. How could I say no? Now, can you remember in the sixties guys wore these very narrow belts? Well, I had one but when I took it off and handed it to her , she discreetly put it on a coat hanger in her closet, but, as she turned she bumped the door open and there was the coat hanger with at least a dozen other belts! My manly ego withered like snot on a doorknob. Yes, my faithful readers – yet another lesson learned.

It puts me in mind of a passage from Robert Swanson's logging poems, in particular the one titled "The Loggers Sweetheart" and I quote:
She walks the street
Her prey to meet
Through bleached blond hair
She hides despair
On the blazing skid roads of sin
And with fond goodbyes
And tears in her eyes
She looks for yet another to skin

DAD KICKS MY PUNK ASS

One day when I was about 14 my father asked me to help get the potatoes dug and picked out of a big field on the farm. First of all, I was a lazy, little, loud-mouthed brat and secondly, I hated work (still do!) and don't like to get my hands dirty. Even today, if I can feel or smell anything on my hands at home or in a restaurant I have to go and wash my hands. It was important to Dad to get the potatoes dug out to sell and feed his big family and time was of the essence as the soil was heavy and forthcoming rain would make it all but impossible to harvest. I, of course, did not understand this or for that matter even care as I was spoiled and an all-round useless tit. I told him there was no money in growing potatoes (I always had an excuse) and I was not going to help. He was patient with me and told me it was a job that had to be done. I just laughed at him and told him I was leaving. He came toward me, so I took off running like a gazelle with Pops in hot pursuit. He was at least 60 and heavy set at 5 feet 8 inches and 210 pounds. I laughed to myself as I thought that there was no way he would ever catch up to me, but , he made a great leap and tripped me as he hooked my left ankle with his. Down I crashed in the black loam, dust flying! As I attempted to get up, he kicked me right up my old address. Keep in mind that he was a good soccer player and played on a number of distinguished soccer teams in his mining days. I must have been catapulted or rather bootapulted about 10 feet! I immediately saw the need in harvesting spuds. To this day I have never had hemorrhoids as I believe they are wedged up around my ears.

THE CHAPERONE

I was the youngest of the 8 children in our family and there was also another Catholic family in Chemainus that had about the same number of kids. My parents were good friends with them and I think that it was expected that one in our family would eventually marry one of theirs. Their father was of French Canadian extraction, and was a very bright man, that had invented sawmill machinery but got cheated out of money promised by the large company that he worked for. The mother was English. Over time, the families whittled down to me being the only one unmarried and they had 2 daughters unwed. One was blond and somewhat busty and the other was dark haired and petite. Both were lookers as we used to call them.

Their parents brought them to the farm one Sunday after mass and the game was on. They brought along one of their sons as well and it was so that he could chaperone me and one of his sisters as we went for a stroll around the farm "160 acres". The poor brother was embarrassed by all of this but in those days you friggin well did what you were told. Anyway the three of us walked down the road but as we got closer to the outbuildings the brother mercifully slowed down as we walked behind the barn that was out of view of the farmhouse. Once behind the barn we stopped and I kissed her, then we turned around and met her brother back on the road. Talk about Speedy Gonzales! The next weekend my parents visited her parents and this young lady and I were talking in the rumpus room downstairs. The mother was very friendly, but kept peeking around the corner so no opportunity arose to sneak in another kiss. Nothing ever developed, but I bet none of you readers have ever been chaperoned on a date.

Robin

The kindest and prettiest girl in Jr High

"DODIE"
AS CLOSE TO A SAINT
AS I HAVE EVER KNOWN

My brother Ken (the firstborn) in our big family married a girl of Dutch extraction who lived in Victoria. Her name was Theodore Gubbels but we all called her Dodie. When I was a boy of about 13, Little Anthony "Bortolotto" thought that we could get rich as songwriters but we knew nothing of a proper composition. We had the words and the tune but that was all. The name of the song was "Then We Can Be Together". We wanted to go on the Talent Caravan, a CBC TV show that traveled across Canada looking for young talent. a 1959 version of Canada's got talent. We approached Dodie as she could compose and was indeed a very talented musician. In spite of having 7 young kids, she always made a little time for us and encouraged us. We practiced the song for a long time but the show decided to skip coming

- 103 -

to Vancouver Island (so like the CBC to this day). We were so disappointed.

Dodie would not tell a lie if it meant her life. No matter how screwed up a person was she always offered them another chance to redeem themselves. When anyone questioned her about it she would look them in the eyes and say, "what do you think Jesus would do?" I remember toward the end she developed brain cancer and was unable to play the organ at St. Peter's as she had done for 50 years.

(63 yrs in total counting Sacred Heart Church in Victoria…all volunteer….)

I went over to see her after mass and she could not make it down the stairs to the after mass gathering for coffee in the church basement without my help. Once she was comfortably seated she was all smiles. I went to the men's room and cried as it just floored me to see this incredibly mentally and physically strong woman this frail. The last time I saw her alive was at New York Pizza as I invited her and her brother Joseph to lunch after a mass. We had a lot of laughs even though she knew she only had a short time left on this earth. When her brother Joe, who she adored, got up to leave to continue on with his incredible life long work for the poor people of Peru "a book in itself", I saw the look in her eyes as she said goodbye to him knowing it was the last time she would ever see him. She maintained her stoicism as did her brother Joe, both as firm in their belief in Jesus and life hereafter as any human could be. I could never say enough about her character and my respect for her.